Praise for the Book

An excellent translation of a necessary work whose great benefit is that it shows Muslims who naturally (like myself) love and practise martial sports that they integrate them to their religious life, and indeed benefit from them spiritually.

HRH Prince Ghazi bin Muhammed
Author of The Sacred Origins of Sports & Culture, *Oxford, UK*

This book is a great read, providing interesting narrations of the Prophet 鶴 and his Companions wrestling each other and staying strong. May it be a means to encourage our youth to adopt the way of the Prophet 鶴, avoid modern technological distractions, remain strong, healthy and follow in the footsteps of the Salaf.

Shaykh Abdur-Raheem Limbada
Tafseer-Raheemi.com, Darul Uloom Bury, UK

The great Imam Abdul Wahhāb al-Sha'rānī 鏡 in "The Muhammadan Contracts" references martial arts (*ālāt al-ji-hād*) as a contract between God and His Messenger 鶴 (and by extension all Muslims) that has become neglected. This important addition to the Islamic English library, Imam Suyūṭī's *al-Musārʿah*, is an endeavour to give life to this neglected Sunna. May it be from amongst the good works of all those involved in this noble endeavour. Amīn.

Shaykh Faiz Qureshy
The Ribat Institute, Surrey, UK

Few athletes are able to put to paper their passion and zeal for the discipline that they are involved in. Ustadh Nisar has successfully brought to light the Islamic basis for undertaking the discipline of wrestling as well as delving into its origins and history amongst Muslims. To my limited knowledge, it is the first book in the English language on the subject of wrestling in Islam and is well overdue. The addition of Imam Suyūṭī's compilation truly enriches the book, making it a must-read for any wrestling enthusiast.

SHAYKH YUSUF BEMATH

Author of Al-ʿAsl, The Pure-bred Arabian Horse, *Port Elizabeth, South Africa*

Many grappling and wrestling books are just dedicated to the technical fundamentals of the fight, thus leaving a gap—in what in my opinion is a flaw in the origin of history and evolution of the sport. *Prophetic Grappling* shows the importance of wrestling and grappling in the battles of the Muslim past and its importance today. For me, as a lover of grappling, in particular Brazilian Jiu-Jitsu, *Prophetic Grappling* is indispensable in my library.

MARIO "SUKATA" NETO

Former UFC fighter, Liverpool, UK

I love learning about the historic significance of grappling throughout the history of humanity as well as the prophetic guidance associated with this beautiful tradition. Thank you Nisar Shaikh for the tremendous research and work you have done on this subject!

ADEM REDZOVIC

Redzovic Jiu-jitsu, Head Instructor, Chicago, USA

This book provides an excellent overview of the ancient Islamic methods and practices pertaining to the art of self-defence. The historic encounter between the Prophet ﷺ and the champion wrestler Rukanah is brought to life via multiple chains of narration documented by Imam Suyūṭī. The modern world, to its detriment, has adopted an increasingly sedentary lifestyle. However, this short treatise highlights that the Islamic tradition has always emphasised physical activity and sports to nurture the mind, body, and soul. A must-read for all students of knowledge, sports, and wrestling enthusiasts.

SAJID HUSSAIN

Chair of The Muslim Sports Foundation, Birmingham, UK

Between the hands of the reader is an excellent, comprehensive treatise relevant to every Muslim in the 21st century. With grappling and martial arts becoming increasingly popular, it is useful to be exposed to the classical scholarly discussions that took place and the historical relevance of the sport.

An important preface to this discussion is the diversity in martial art forms. While striking and injuring tends to be the focus in some, resistance and technique is the focus in others. Grappling falls into the latter category where the trainee is taught to engage with full resistance from the first day. This basic point fosters an appreciation in the mind of the reader, of the similarity between modern-day grappling and the prophetic example, along with the overall Islamic ethos of developing physical strength, discipline and ability. This work has paved the path in offering a well-rounded, well-researched publication on the topic of prophetic grappling in the English language.

MUFTI HUSSAIN KAMANI
Qalam Institute, Texas, USA

The benefits of wrestling—physically, mentally, and spiritually—are not fully realised until one takes to learning this noble art, an art that shows dominance without damage. With every world civilisation having a culture of wrestling, all realising its importance in battle, self-defence, physical strength, and fitness, it is great to finally see a book written on the grappling of the Prophet ﷺ and the Muslims in general.

I would recommend this book in the hope that we take an understanding of the principles and objectives of wrestling by the noble Prophet ﷺ, something that should motivate us to adopt the art as well as being able to apply them in all aspects of life.

LYUBO KUMBAROV
Renowned Wrestling Coach, 4 x Bulgarian National Champion,
Team GB Wrestling Elite Performance Coach

First published in the UK by Beacon Books and Media Ltd
Earl Business Centre, Dowry Street, Oldham OL8 2PF UK.

First edition published in 2022

www.beaconbooks.net

ISBN   978-1-915025-15-9   Paperback

ISBN   978-1-915025-16-6   Hardback

ISBN   978-1-915025-17-3   Ebook

Cataloging-in-Publication record for this book is available from the British Library

Cover created by ArifulHazam (tabassam.desain)

PROPHETIC GRAPPLING

PROPHETIC GRAPPLING

INCLUDING AS-SUYŪTĪ'S

المُسَارَعَةِ إلى المُصَارَعَةِ

AL-MUSĀRʿAH ILA AL-MUṢĀRʿAH
(TRANSLATED BY MUHAMMAD AMAN HAQUE)

NISAR SHAIKH

BEACON BOOKS

Contents

ACKNOWLEDGEMENTS

We learn from the Prophet Muhammad ﷺ that if we fail to thank people, we fail to thank God. This work was a collaboration of many people.

May God bless and reward with abundance the learned Reviver, Traditionalist, Jurist, our Master Imam Jalāl Ad-Dīn as-Suyūṭi (God have mercy upon him) for the immense service he has rendered the religion of Islam, a testimony to his sincerity and acceptance with God is that centuries later, we are still being enlightened by his noble works.

We thank the venerable Shaykh Muḥammad ibn ʿAlawi al Mālikī (God have mercy on him) for his lofty, courageous, and sincere contributions in all the Islamic sciences of this Ummah and his righteous student, Shaykh Seraj Hendricks (God have mercy upon him) for his teachings and writing a short yet insightful article years ago which laid clear perhaps what has been amiss from the Muslims for generations.

I would like to thank Imam Zaid Shakir for giving me his precious time for an entire morning on a bright November Friday outside Zaytuna College, California. His humility, joviality, kind words and encouragement to see a translation of this work has carried me ever since.

I am deeply grateful to my teacher, Shaykh Ibrahim Osi-Efa for his encouragement, review of the initial draft and sincere advice, as well as my dear teacher and brother, Shaykh Thaqib Mahmood for introducing me to the work of Imām as-Suyūṭī.

Special thanks to Ustadh Saleh Malik for his continued encouragement, without whom this work would have remained unfinished on a hard drive somewhere; Shaykh Gibril Fouad Haddad for his correspondence and clarifications; Mufti Muhammad Aman Haque for rendering the original translation; Mufti Abdur Rahman Mangera for his encouragement and imparting a little of his immense knowledge of books and publishing; Imam Dawud Walid for his time clarifying details around Blackness and Islam; Shaykh Uwais Namazi for retyping and vowelizing the original Arabic text, and Shaykh Muhammad Husain Kazi for reviewing and editing the original translation.

A huge thank you to Maulana Asim Ayyub and Maulana Syed Saquib Ahmed for their research around the various Rukānah ahadith, the history and narrations of the water of Zam Zam, providing the references to the forms of Satan in the Qur'an and ahadith and their translation of an excerpt of *Silat al-Riyāda* of Shaykh Muḥammad ibn ʿAlawi. Their contributions, thoughts and scholarship are immeasurable assets to the Muslims of Britain.

I thank all my teachers in the grappling arts, for their knowledge and willingness to teach. I thank every single one of my dear students for their support and desire to see a work of this nature come to fruition, along with my fellow trustees at Noah's Ark charity for facilitating elements of this work. To all my dear friends in the UK (you know who you are) and in Canada (you know who you are) for their valuable input and positivity.

I am deeply grateful to our teacher, the unfaltering scholar and caller from the Prophetic house, Habīb Kāẓim as-Saqqāf for his encouragement, good opinion and writing the foreword. Likewise, may God reward and bless my brother, Habib Shroufi, for his continued help, patience, and persistence.

I am ever grateful to my brother, Gulam Mohammed, my sister, Nazia and my dear parents, Mohammed Firoz and Khatija

Bibi, whose unconditional love, support and beautiful ways will always serve me as lasting examples of the Prophetic model. I thank my boys, Musa, Muadh, Abdur-Raheem and Anas, for their encouraging words (and mumbles), their desire to finally see "Daddy's book" and for whom I pray that they follow the example of the Chosen One ﷺ in all they endeavour to do.

And lastly, gratitude to my lifeline, soul mate and beloved wife, Saba, for her useful suggestions, patience, encouragement, love, and support, without whom this book would never have come to be.

Nisar Ahmed Shaikh
London, UK
Rabīʿ al-Awwal 1442 | November 2020

ABOUT THE AUTHORS

COMPILER

'Abd Ar-Raḥmān ibn Abū Bakr ibn Muhammad ibn Sābiq ad-Dīn, more commonly known as the celebrated Jalāl Ad-Dīn as-Suyūṭī ﷺ, the prolific and legendary ninth century Egyptian scholar born in 849AH. Although born in Cairo, his attribution to the ancient city of Asyūṭ came from his father who migrated to the modern capital.

From a scholarly family, as-Suyūṭī inherited an extensive family library which fed his inquisitive nature and nurtured the polymath and prolific author he was to become. He memorised the Qur'an by age 8 and all the standard books of Arabic grammar and Islamic jurisprudence. His impressive scholarly output remains with over 600 titles to his name, many of which are encyclopaedic in nature and cover nearly all aspects of the Islamic tradition. He travelled extensively around the Muslim world to gather the traditions of the Messenger of God ﷺ, visiting Morocco, Syria, Hijaz, Yemen and India.

He was considered by many as the reviver (*Mujaddid*) of the 9th century who passed away in 911AH buried next to his father in Asyūṭ.[1]

---

[1] Adapted from several biographies; see Imam Jalal Ad-Din as-Suyūṭī, *Al-Arba'īn – On the Principles of Legal Judgements, Virtuous Actions, and Asceticism,* (Turath Publishing, 2009) and Al-Suyūṭī by GF Haddad (https://www.livingislam.org/suyuti_e.html)

ANNOTATED BY

Nisar Ahmed Shaikh is an avid grappler having trained extensively in Jiu-jitsu and cross trained in freestyle and Greco-style Wrestling, Judo and Sambo. He holds a 2nd Degree Black Belt in Jiu-jitsu under the Carlson Gracie Team London. His passion for the grappling arts has taken him abroad, seeking out instruction from some of the best grapplers in the world, visiting Brazil, Japan, USA and Canada. He is a deeply passionate and active teacher with over eighteen years' experience, instructing all levels, from professional MMA fighters to young children. He currently serves as a Muslim Chaplain at Royal Holloway University in London, where he lives with his family.

TRANSLATED BY

Mufti Mohammad Aman Haque initiated his Islamic studies in 2003 at Jamia Uloom al-Islamiyya in Toronto, Canada. He then completed his BA in Islamic Sciences and Arabic Literature (*Alimiyyah*) at Jamia Talim al-Islam Institute in Dewsbury, UK. He attained a Diploma in Contextual Islamic Studies and Leadership at the Cambridge Muslim College in Cambridge, UK as well as completing a Specialisation Studies programme in Islamic Jurisprudence (*Fiqh & Ifta*) at the Markaz ad-Dawat al Islamiyyah Center of Higher Islamic Research in Dhaka, Bangladesh. He is currently completing his MA in Arabic at the University of Bergen, Norway.

FOREWORD

In the Name of God, Most Merciful, Most Clement.

All praise belongs to God, the Magnanimous and Merciful, amongst whose glorious names are the All-Mighty, Strong and Dominant (*al-Qawi, al-Jabbār, al-Muhaymin*).

I bear witness there is no deity and Lord except Him and that our Master Muhammad ﷺ is His bondsman and Messenger. May God bless him and all other Prophets and Messengers, along with our Prophet's ﷺ progeny and Companions.

Islamic wrestling, by which is meant wrestling per the Islamic code of conduct and practice, is amongst the most important sports and exercise (*riyadhat*) in Islam, and via which a Muslim develops the strength and endurance to obey God and strive in His path.

It is enough of an honour and privilege for Muslim grapplers who observe the Islamic code of conduct that the most beloved, our great Prophet ﷺ, grappled. He grappled with Rukanah ibn 'Abd Yazid ⵁ which subsequently resulted in his conversion to Islam, as reported in a *hasan* narration. Similarly, two Companions of the Prophet ﷺ, Samurah ibn Jundub ⵁ and Rafi' ibn Khadij ⵁ grappled too. The former was an excellent grappler and the latter a distinguished archer. May God be pleased with all the Prophet's ﷺ Companions.

My dear brother in Islam and, God willing, companion in Paradise, Nisar Shaikh has had the work of Imam al-Suyūṭī, titled *Al-Musār'ah ilā al-Muṣār'ah*, translated with an interest to promote this sunnah of the most beloved Prophet ﷺ pertaining to the ancient and luminous art of Islamic grappling.

May God reward him handsomely and bless his endeavour. May this work be recorded in his register of good deeds and counted amongst the beneficial knowledge whose reward continues to pay dividends after death.

May it benefit contemporary Muslim generations and those to come.

Lastly, may this work prove a strong cause in the triumph of truth and this religion, in the spread of the Islamic teachings (*Shariah*) and, more importantly, the character of the Prophet ﷺ in all spheres of life and under all circumstances. Āmīn.

[Al-Habīb] Kāẓim ibn Ja'far as-Saqqāf Bā 'Alawī
(God protect and preserve him)

Tarim, Yemen
Dar al-Mustafa
Rabi al-Thani, 1443AH

INTRODUCTION

لَّقَدْ كَانَ لَكُمْ فِى رَسُولِ ٱللَّهِ أُسْوَةٌ حَسَنَةٌ لِّمَن كَانَ يَرْجُوا ٱللَّهَ وَٱلْيَوْمَ

ٱلْءَاخِرَ وَذَكَرَ ٱللَّهَ كَثِيرًا. ۞ ٣٣:٢١

There has certainly been for you in the Messenger of God an
excellent example for anyone whose hope is in God and the
Last Day and [who] remembers God often. (Qur'an, 33:21)

In the name of God, the Compassionate, the Merciful.

Praise be to God, Lord of all the Worlds. Peace and blessings
upon His Noble Messenger, our Master Muhammad, his family,
his Companions and all those who follow in their way.

The personage of Muhammad, the Messenger of God ﷺ,
is an immense and lofty one. Many are naturally selective of
the Prophetic practices they imbibe in their lives, choosing to
implement those that are best suited to their own capacity, af-
finity and ultimately the ones that are most beneficial to them.
Yet, adopting even the slightest facet of his ﷺ way would bring
about the greatest blessing and direction in our lives. This can
be witnessed every year on the day of Hajj, when the followers
of the greatest of God's creation gather on the plains of Arafat
in all their colours and backgrounds, in a moment of profound
strength and beauty. There, the way (*Sunnah*) of the Messenger of
God ﷺ can be seen in the cab driver from Marrakech, the nurse
from Kuala Lumpur, the farmer from South Africa, the scholar

from India, the book keeper from London and the restaurateur from San Francisco.

Muslims relish and endeavour to fulfil every Prophetic practice, from his ﷺ eating, sitting, engaging with the poor, dress, conduct with his womenfolk, even to the very method by which he would relieve himself ﷺ. Islamic literature is replete with examples covering every conceivable aspect of his ﷺ life, the very preservation of which is testimony to his ﷺ position with God, the noble rank he ﷺ has been uniquely allotted as well as the love and adherence of his ﷺ followers. Arguably the most documented man in history, it is without doubt that the influence of the life of the Messenger of God ﷺ on enlightening a civilisation is unparalleled in history, spanning great innovation, wisdom and development across spheres as diverse as medicine, mathematics, geometry, astronomy, nutrition, and as the present work will demonstrate, sport.

All civilisations, without exception, enjoy a culture of sport. The origins of these sports may have grown out of circumstances and served specific functions at a given time and place. Noble arts such as archery, swordsmanship, equitation and wrestling were the established "sports" at the time of the Messenger of God ﷺ. Whilst this topic of the "Sport of the Prophet ﷺ" has been elaborated upon by the great scholars of previous generations, at a time where the frivolity of modern sports culture and increasingly distracting technology endanger the future health and quite often the faith of the young, a much-needed call for a "revival" of the Prophetic arts is overdue. Unfortunately, the measure of value and benefit gained from any activity is evaluated far too hastily in the modern age. Evidently, the way in which martial arts and sports are practised now—with a host of weekend warriors and serial "dabblers" seeking momentary combative stardom—is far removed from the disciplined, sustained, and purposeful practice of our pious predecessors and has undoubtedly led to a generation struggling to function, much less lead.[2]

2 Leonard Sax, *Boys Adrift*, (Basic Books, 2007)

Prophetic Grappling touches upon the history of the noble practice of grappling, its practice in the time of the Prophet 鐮 and his Companions, the objectives of sports in Islam more generally, and some of the established benefits one can accrue from its practice. It includes *Al-Musārʿah ilā al-Muṣārʿah* (Swiftly to Wrestling), a short treatise penned by the prolific and esteemed scholar of the 9th Islamic century, Jalāl Ad-Dīn as-Suyūṭī 鐮. This is a short collection of eighteen traditions (*hadith*) and sayings (*āthār*) of the Messenger of God 鐮 and his blessed Companions, mentioning how he 鐮 engaged in the art of wrestling with the dominant fighters of the day; his 鐮 encouraging his beloved Companions to wrestle; incidents in which they wrestled and the consequences his 鐮 wrestling had upon those whom he 鐮 faced. At the time of writing, it is the first translation of the work in English of the Arabic text published by *Maktaba al-Sawādi al-Tawzīʿ* (1413AH/1992).

It is with this intention that a translation of the short tract penned by the illustrious Imam with accompanying notes to identify the objectives of the martial arts in Islam has been rendered.

References for the all the Quranic verses, ahadith and relevant religious texts have been provided in the footnotes or incorporated into the text itself. The translations for the Quranic verses are taken from Mufti Taqi Usmani (*The Noble Qurʾan*, Turath Publishing 2019) and Professor Abdul Haleem (*The Qurʾan – Oxford World's Classics*, OUP, 2008). Excerpts from Shaykh Muhammad ibn Alawi al-Maliki's work *Silat al-Riyādati bil-Dīn wa-Dawruha fi Tanshiʾati al-Shabāb al-Muslim* ("The Relation between Exercise and Religion and its Role in the Development of Muslim Youth", King Fahd National Library, 1st Edition – 1419AH/ 1999) has also been included, broadly establishing for the first time the objectives of sports in Islam, in English.

The present work was originally aimed to serve as supplementary reading for those engaged in the annual Futuwwa Retreat organised by Greensville Trust, UK, under the guidance of one of the UK's truly visionary and commendable scholars, Shaykh Ibrahim Osi-Efa (God protect and preserve him and his family). Through the help of a handful of scholars and martial artists, it has now flourished into a short publication which we hope inspires a generation to turn to the noble example of the Messenger of God ﷺ as it relates to our physical activity.

> It is right to say that the Prophet, upon him blessings and peace, was the apex of *futuwwa*, a word that is both nobler and more inclusive of moral qualities than the modern Arabic word for sport, *riyāda*, which denotes four meanings: youth, virility, bravery, and generosity. Among the ideals subsumed in these four attributes is the modern concept of sportsmanship. (Gibril Fouad Haddad, *Sports in Islam*)

PART I

A History of Grappling in Islamic Civilisation

Wrestling, and by extension grappling[3] in general, has undoubtedly existed since time immemorial. It is arguably the oldest martial form documented by all the major civilisations of the world and has been considered, along with running and lifting, as one of the first forms of physical exercise for humanity. It is an art form which, despite its intensity, is innately expressed by young children. At the point a child learns to walk, he or she instinctively learns "micro-movements" like knee crawling, crawling on "all-fours", bum-shuffling, spine rocking, turning up and down from the belly, and even the precise way of moving from a standing to a seated position—all precursors to upright and ground grappling. It is through this combination of natural human movement, no requirement of external equipment, and the ability to manipulate the human body that reinforces its claim as the oldest martial art known to man.

As with any historical premise, it is categorically impossible to assert with complete certainty a firm date as to when man first

3 The difference between wrestling and grappling is one related to rules and objectives. One could argue that "wrestling" is a subset of the greater genre of grappling. Put simply, wrestling could be reduced to the art of taking an opponent down and pinning their shoulders to the ground. Grappling, more widely, would include stand-up wrestling but also incorporate the use of submission joint locks, chokes and muscle compressions found in ground-wrestling. Modern wrestling has been limited to two main strands, Freestyle and Greco-Roman, both distinct from each other in which techniques are permitted and have been Olympic sports since their introduction in 1900. Other grappling arts such as Sambo, Judo and Jiu-jitsu, adding the complexity of a "Gi" (grappling jacket and trousers) with their myriad variations and rulesets, broadly make up the remaining "Grappling genre", introduce further techniques in tripping, throwing, joint-locking and choking. The remaining grappling arts, of which Ruadhan Macfadden (https://thousandholds.net/product/grappling-around-the-world-map-download/) who took on the commendable task of tracing as many grappling art forms from around the world as he could, finally arriving at 74 (albeit excluding the whole of the Arabian Peninsula), share mostly or in part in some form to the above mentioned. Objectives, rulesets, attire, and reward differ quite dramatically.

lay his hands on another and began to tussle, control, take down, pin and submit. But ancient stone inscriptions, illustrations and historical accounts have alluded to human grappling as early as 3000BC.[4] Many hold wrestling as the first "social" exercise, unlike running (solo activity) and lifting (stones, spears, etc.) which require no other participants.

The verb "to wrestle" (صرع) connotes two primary definitions in the Arabic language:

i.   take part in a fight, either as sport or in earnest, that involves grappling with one's opponent and trying to throw or force them to the ground.
ii. Struggle with a difficulty or problem.

Whilst we are more concerned in this book with the former definition, its secondary meaning resonates with the nature of our existence in this world.

God reminds us:

$$\text{٢٩:٦٩ ۞ وَٱلَّذِينَ جَٰهَدُواْ فِينَا لَنَهْدِيَنَّهُمْ سُبُلَنَا ۚ}$$

And those who struggle for Us, We will surely guide them to our ways. (Qur'an, 29:69)

One's guidance from God is inextricably linked to struggle. Nothing of value is attained without it. An immediate outcome of learning the art of wrestling is a type of methodology for dealing with struggle or more appropriately, strife.

---

4 Michael B. Poliakoff, *Combat Sports in the Ancient World,* (Yale University Press, 1995), 1–2.

In Arabia

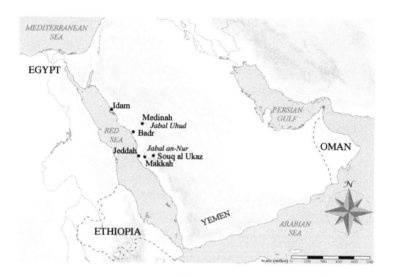

Map of the Arabian Peninsula[5]

In contrast to the historical accounts of wrestling in other parts of the world, the history of grappling in the Arabian Peninsula is comparatively scarce. Aside from the definitive narrations of the Prophet Muhammad ﷺ brought forward by Imam as-Suyūṭī, as detailed in the present work, documentation of wrestling specifically is limited. However, what has been

5 Map produced by Thomas Bachrach, July 2021.

8

established is that grappling was a significant part of the culture amongst Arab men and youth at the time of Islam and prior.

> Wrestling was a popular pastime among the boys of Arabia, and they frequently fought each other. There was no malice in these fights. It was a sport, and boys were trained in wrestling as one of the requirements of Arab manhood.[6]

This is particularly significant given the harsh and rugged nature of the Arab Bedouin, who led difficult lives contending with the arid and harsh desert environment. The men around the Messenger of God ﷺ were Bedouin Arabs, given to fighting and fending off raids against their property and people. "Raiding and fighting, as well as defending themselves against raids, were an integral part of their lives."[7] Arabian culture was one of deep ancestral pride and tribal conflicts.[8] Alexander the Great—arguably the greatest conqueror in recorded history—despite creating a dedicated navy to gather intelligence on this unknown land, dispatching three naval missions and colonising parts of the coastal areas of Eastern Arabia,[9] failed in conquering such a hardy people in a hostile land.

The formation of a military force in the conventional sense, with efforts to organise, train and gather soldiers, would only exist in essentially "non-military and civilian societies" where a military arm to defend a people would be necessary. This was not the case for early Islam and arguably not even something reflected upon by the Arabs at that time, as *"with few marginal exceptions, all adult males were fighters"* and it was only after the Islamic conquests of neighbouring lands that they developed more structured approaches to formulating an army and military socialisation.

6 A.I. Akram, *Sword of Allāh – Khalid bin al-Waleed*, (Maktabah Publishers & Distributors, 2004), p.1.
7 Hugh Kennedy, *The Armies of the Caliphs*, (Routledge, 2001).
8 Albert Hourani, *A History of the Arab Peoples*, (Faber & Faber Ltd, 1991).
9 Daniel T. Potts, *The Arabian Gulf in Antiquity: Volume II: From Alexander the Great to the Coming of Islam*, (Oxford University Press, 1990).

> The military forces lacked any system of remuneration,
> fighting as they did for booty, honour or self-defence.
> Nor did they have any structure of command with
> coercive powers. There were certainly tribal nobles, the
> *ashrāf* (sing., *sharīf*), who owed their status to descent
> and their own abilities, but they were obeyed only
> voluntarily. The individual bedouin tent preserved its
> own autonomy, just as it provided its own subsistence
> and the warrior his own weapons. Social identity,
> formal training, providing equipment and payment,
> all characteristics of a true army, were foreign to this
> society.[10]

Under these strained circumstances, the need to be strong, fit
and able to fight was imperative. Militarily, the advantages the
early Muslims possessed "were simply those of mobility, good
leadership and, perhaps most important of all, motivation and
high morale."[11]

There are a great number of books written on medieval Arabic
military which, albeit limited in detail, make mention of the
martial methods of the Muslim armies. They detail the strategies
used, military discipline, leadership characteristics, mobilisation
and ambush techniques of the various dynasties of Islam from
the time of the Prophet 🕌 and subsequent caliphs within Arabia,
to the conquests of Iraq and Persia in the East, and Syria, Egypt
and North Africa in the West.

> After the conquest of Spain, the Arabs had already
> built a vast empire extending from the Atlantic shores
> to the Indus in about one hundred years. While the
> Arabs began to develop their warfare system they did
> not disdain to learn many lessons from the nations they
> already defeated... Arab writers and translators began

---

10 Ibid.
11 Hugh Kennedy, *The Great Arab Conquests: How Islam Changed the World We Live In*, (Da Capo
Press, 2008).

to contribute invaluable treatises on war, archery and chivalry.[12]

Sadly, few of these treatises survived but it was a well-established fact that "by the tenth century, the Arabs had an art of war of their own." For instance, it was commonplace at the beginning of a battle for individual duels to the death to take place, which would occasionally serve to nullify the entire conflict.

The ability to grapple was imperative in close-quarters combat, which was frequently the case in early battles. With only occasional use of horses or camels, foot soldiers made up most of the fighting force. It was the actions of these brave souls who possessed such limited weaponry,[13] that would often be the deciding factor in the outcome of the engagement.

> They would throw away their spears and fight with swords, often ending up by wrestling their opponents to the ground.[14]

Thus, a significant part of the training of the soldiers of each generation was the requirement to learn wrestling and grappling techniques.

In light of the various grappling forms in the world with their unique histories, rules and currency, it begs the question: what style and form of grappling did the Messenger of God ﷺ practise?

Judging by the prevalent martial forms present in and around the Arabian peninsula, the narrations brought to us by Imam as-Suyūṭī and the wrestling styles documented from antiquity, we can confidently assert that the style practised around the time of the Prophet ﷺ was a culmination of predominantly

---

12 A. Rahman Zaky, *A Preliminary Bibliography of Medieval Arabic Military Literature*, (Consejo Superior de Investigaciones Científicas, 1965).
13 During the Battle of Uhud, with the Quraysh firing arrows upon the Muslims, the masterful archer, Sa'd ibn Abi Waqās reused an enemy arrow killing his opponent. The same arrow was shot back at him, Sa'd once again reshot the arrow killing a second opponent. Once again, the same arrow was shot back to Sa'd, who for the third time reshot the arrow killing a third opponent. Astonished at this amazing feat of archery in war, Sa'd reveals that each of the retrieved arrows were given to him by none other than the Prophet ﷺ. Ibn Asākir; recorded in Muhammad Yusuf Kandhlawi, *Hayatus Sahabah – The Lives of the Sahabah, Vol.1* (Islamic Book Service, 2010), p.531.
14 Ibid.

cross standing wrestling styles—between modern-day freestyle[15] and Greco-Roman style wrestling[16]—with a fell and/or pinning of the shoulders constituting victory, as well as a small degree of ground grappling.[17]

However, it is altogether difficult to affirm with certainty that this was the only grappling form known. This is partly due to its primary role in military combat where the use of submission locks, holds and pins would have undoubtedly proved indispensable.

In Arabia, grappling would not only serve as a gauge for military fitness,[18] but also as selection criteria for leadership and quashing rivalries. Contemporary sources on combat sports assert that the Arabian Peninsula inherited wrestling from the great wrestling civilisation of Nubia (modern-day Sudan) and Egypt.[19]

By all accounts, it would be difficult to find a "slouch" amongst the Companions of the Messenger of God ﷺ, who collectively took every opportunity to train and ready themselves for battle at a moment's notice.

---

15 In freestyle wrestling, wrestlers can take a wide variety of holds on both the upper body and legs, but may not grasp the opponent's clothing to secure a hold, with the objective of pinning their opponent's shoulders to the ground or outscoring them through the execution of takedowns and/or turnovers.
16 Similar to freestyle wrestling with the exception that Greco-Roman rules do not permit holds below the waist.
17 See Part IV, Narration 5 of the present text.
18 See Part IV, Narration 10 of the present text.
19 Carroll, "Wrestling in Ancient Nubia", 20.

In the Sanctuaries

Mecca at the time of the Prophet ﷺ was a bustling yet hostile environment. Traders would viciously vie with each other over selling their own intricate craft works, plump livestock and sweet delicacies to the locals and visiting pilgrims from different lands, to fulfil their cherished desire to visit the House of God. Horse and camel carts were dragged along by their weathered masters, who toiled the land for produce in the blistering heat by day, and were capable archers and formidable fighters by night.

In contrast, Medīnah was a lush and opulent city, with abundant gardens, water wells and copious date produce. The forced displacement of the Prophet ﷺ and his followers to this city provided much-needed relief from the persecution they faced in Mecca at the hands of the Quraysh. The Prophet ﷺ along with his indefatigable Companions ؓ, following an epic twelve-day sojourn through Arabia—leaving 26 Safar and arriving 12 Rabi' al-Awwal, upon the commencement of the Islamic calendar—and despite being uprooted from their home and for many, their birthplace, continued to work to restore their livelihoods, remained committed to their faith and diligent with their daily martial practices.

Following the inauguration of the first mosque established by the Prophet ﷺ in Quba, a new and revitalised sanctuary was established in Medīnah less than three miles away.

> He ﷺ stayed for six months in the house of Abū Ayyub al-Ansāri ؓ of the Bani Najjar tribe until his own house, built on the eastern side of the newly constructed mosque, was finished. When the mosque was originally built, it was 1,050 square meters and was more than doubled to 2,500 square meters in the seventh year of the Hijrah.
>
> The pulpit in the Prophet's Mosque in Medīnah now stands on the exact location where the Prophet ﷺ originally stopped upon his arrival in Medīnah.[20]

Contrary to the normative states of mosques today which are often under-utilised, embroiled in sectarianism and which many youth and women find unwelcoming, the Prophet's mosque *Masjid an-Nabawi* was a bustling hub of activity alongside its primary function as a place of worship for the Muslims. The initial structure of the Prophet's ﷺ mosque was a basic one as described:

> The mosque was a picture of simplicity, free from every kind of elaboration. The walls were made of unbaked bricks, the palm-leaf roof stood over pillars of palm-tree trunks. The *qiblah* was in the direction of the Bayt-al-Maqdis (Jerusalem) but when it was changed to the Ka'ba (Mecca) a new door was made on the northern side. The floor was left to its natural unpaved state. The result was that when it rained, the floor became muddy and sticky. Once, the Companions brought with them pebbles which they spread on their individual places. The Prophet ﷺ was pleased with that and had the entire floor covered with pebbles.[21]

---

20 Abdullah H. Al-Kadi, *Mecca to Medīnah – A Photographic Journey of the Hijrah Route*, (Orient East, 2013).
21 Shibli Nomani & Syed S. Nadwi, *Sirat-un-Nabi – Life of the Prophet*, (Darul Ishaat, 2003) p.231.

An honoured space was established within the mosque, known as the blessed *Rawdah,* an area located between the house of the Prophet's wife Ā'isha and the pulpit. It was at this revered spot—commonly referred to as "a garden from the gardens of paradise"—that the Companions were found shooting arrows and wrestling, whilst the Prophet 鐙 looked on with approval.

The famed incident of the Abyssinians' demonstration of martial spearplay in front of the Prophet 鐙 within its confines, led to scholars commenting on the multifaceted function of the mosque:

> This indulgence on the part of the Prophet 鐙 in permitting and encouraging such sport in his Mosque was to demonstrate that the Mosque serves both worldly and religious purposes. Muslims congregate in the Mosque not only to worship but also to play. However, this play is not to be merely for fun but should involve physical exercise and training. Commenting on this hadith (of the Abyssinians), scholars have said that the Mosque is the centre of the Muslims' community affairs, and any activity which combines benefits for religion and for the Muslims may be carried out in it. Muslims of the present time should note how devoid mosques today are of vitality and strength, often having become havens for the elderly and the lazy.[22]

Eligibility to participate in military campaigns was a matter of concern. With limited weaponry, cavalry and resources, subjecting the already fledgling Muslim community to the hordes of Quraysh in battle was not something to be taken lightly.

An "annual grappling examination" of the young Companions 鐙 amongst the Helpers (*Ansār*) was undertaken by the Messenger of God 鐙 himself, with eager men being pitted against each other in highly competitive bouts to ensure the fittest were ready for battle.

---

22 Yusuf al-Qaradawi, *The Lawful and The Prohibited in Islam,* (Al-Birr Foundation, 2003), p.272.

Barely a kilometre northwest of the Prophet's mosque, now by *Masjid as-Sabāq*, lay a dusty portion of land used for combat training and horse racing, which also signified the starting point of a ten-kilometre racecourse upon which horse rehearsal drills took place.[23]

As was common with most grappling that took place in antiquity, the sands of the Arabian desert provided plentiful opportunities to hone technique and settle rivalries. The most famous was the *Souq-al 'Ukāz* (Market of Okāz), a place known amongst pre-Islamic Arabs for the exchanging of ideas, poetry festivals (and showdowns), storytelling, entertaining performances, and displays of strength. The captivating bout between the Messenger of God ﷺ and Rukānah took place at Idam, which according to the celebrated historian, *Jarīr al-Tabari*, is located at the present *Wādi al-Hamd*, which enters the Red Sea 50 kilometres south of *al-Wajh* in north-western Arabia.[24]

---

23   Muhammad Ilyas Abdul Ghani, *Pictorial History of Medīnah Munawwarah*, (Al-Rasheed Printers, 2004).
24   Jarir al-Tabari, *History of al-Tabari ,Vol.8,* Translated by Michael Fishbein, (State University of New York Press, 1997) p.151.

Across the Muslim World

Undoubtedly, the greatest and most well-preserved contribution to wrestling as a combat art has been made by the nation of Persia (modern-day Iran). Of all the available sources on wrestling in the Muslim world, by far the most comprehensive and detailed descriptions are captured in Persian anthropology, with traditions relating to Sham, son of the Prophet Nūh 🕮 being a skilled wrestler. The epic *Shahnameh,* written by the Persian poet Ferdowsi, describes warriors wrestling after their "swords, lances and maces had broken."[25] Subsequent poetic literature like the *Garshasp-nama* (Book of Garshasp) by Asadi Tusi and *Zafar-nama* (Book of Victories) by Hamdollah Mostowfi similarly provide inspirational verses pertaining to the culture of wrestling at the time. A renowned manual, *Adab al-Harb va al-Shoja-e* (Customs of War and Bravery) written by Fakr-al-dīn Mohammad b. Manṣūr Mobārakšā also detailed wrestling techniques specific to application in warfare.[26]

It is Persian culture's longstanding reverence for the warrior tradition that has contributed to its preservation of martial arts history, inspirational poetry and continued excellence in the art

25 Khorasani, M. M, *Persian Archery and Swordsmanship: Historical Martial Arts of Iran,* (Niloufer Books, 2013); contains an immensely rich catalogue of wrestling history.
26 Thomas A. Green, *Martial Arts of the World: An Encyclopedia of History and Innovation, Vol. 2* (ABC-CLIO, 2010).

of wrestling. The traditional *Zoorkhanes* (Houses of Strength) are still maintained and active to this day, providing communities of young boys, men and the elderly a space within which to develop "strength, endurance, and training using traditional methods, not only in physical techniques but also in moral values and etiquette."[27] Most *Zoorkhanes* are built around a wrestling pit, with exercise led by a *miydander* as appointed by a *Murshid* (an Elder leading the gym). Classical training equipment like the *sang* (weighted shields), *takhte-ye shena* (wooden plank typically used for sword training) and the *meel* (weighted clubs) are used interchangeably to strengthen the body in specific and wrestling-relevant protocols.

Even modern-day Iran is a grappling nation. Millions of its youth actively wrestle and many compete globally at all levels and within various styles of grappling, ranging from freestyle, Greco-Roman and an ancient style known as *Chookheh* (taken from the name of the woollen jacket worn) which bears similarities with Jiu-jitsu, with fighters wearing woollen jackets without sleeves, belts and trousers reaching the knees.

Another traditional Persian grappling style more widely practised in the Northern Iranian provinces along the Caspian Sea is *Gileh-Mardi*. This style places particular emphasis on opening ceremonial rituals including stepping towards and standing in the direction of Mecca and ritualising the Arabian battle tradition of walking into the field of a bout, asking for an opponent. The opponent may opt to take on the bout or refuse and leave the field. The loser is he who touches the ground with a knee or even a finger. Interestingly, there are over twenty documented styles of grappling found in Iran, each with slightly varied rules, starting positions, initiation ceremonies and prizes.[28]

It is narrated that during the caliphate of Mu'āwiyah ﷺ, the Roman Emperor had sent two herculean athletes—one being

27 Ibid.
28 For further details, refer to Sarrafi, "The Way of Traditional Persian Wrestling Styles," 4–10.

particularly tall and wide, the other powerfully built with an immense grip—to measure their strength against the soldiers of the Muslim army. Upon consulting 'Amr ibn al-'Aas ﷺ, it was decided that Qays, son of the Companion, Sa'd ibn Ubāda ﷺ would battle with the tall one and Muhammad ibn Ḥanafiyya,[29] son of 'Alī ibn Abī Ṭālib ﷺ, with the Roman powerhouse. As the Caliph and other dignitaries took their seats, the powerhouse walked across the field meeting Muhammad ibn Hanafiyya face to face. The challenge was set—each man would extend their arm out whilst remaining seated and resist being pulled up by his opponent. The Roman opting to be first, grabbed the arm of Muhammad ibn Hanafiyya as he sat fixed on the ground. Despite his efforts, the Roman was unable to move Muhammad from his place and acknowledged his weakness. Then Muhammad took his turn and with a dynamic jerk, immediately lifted the Roman into the air and threw him to the ground.[30]

During the Abbasid dynasty, there was a resurgence of physical and sporting culture with the caliphate's capital Baghdad hosting lengthy horse tracks (*maydāns*), horse polo, running, wrestling and archery. The sixth Abbasid caliph, Amīn al-Rashīd, was a man who enjoyed physical exercise and famously wrestled a lion, illustrating the centrality the art enjoyed throughout the ages. Years later, at the time of the Buyid caliph al-Mustakfī, wrestling tournaments were held in public squares along with swimming races in the Tigris River, leading to Buyid emir, Mui'zz al-Dawla, hosting regular wrestling competitions.

> Wrestling matches of the 4th/10th century held at the bidding of the Buwayhid Mu'izz al-Dawla at Baghdad present a remarkable scene. On the day of the wrestling competition a tree was set up in the race-course (*maydan*) with prizes containing valuable things

---

29 Muhammad 'Alī ibn Abī Ṭālib later known has Muhammad ibn Hanafiyya, was born in Medīnah in 15AH/ 637AD and was the third son of the 'Alī ibn Abī Talib. His mother was Khawlah bint Ja'far from the Banu Hanifa tribe, whom 'Alī married after the death of Fatimah ﷺ.
30 *Suwār min Hayāt Tabi'īn* – Dr. Abdur Rahman Ra'fat Basha (Daar al-Adab al-Islami, 1997).

hanging thereon purses of dirhams were also placed at the feet of the tree. Musicians with drums and flutes made the occasion colourful. The contest continued for hours and the winners received rewards and robes of honour from Mui'zz al-Dawla.[31]

The attire of grapplers differed from region to region, reasons for which no doubt depended much on the climate of the land, people's custom of dress, clothing material availability, societal affluence, the style of grappling established and subsequent evolution. It is interesting to note the degree to which practitioners would even abandon cultural and religious demands with the aim of fulfilling the art's objectives. Examples of devoutly religious men, donning fortified loincloths and freely exposing their bodies seemed part of the spectacle.

Other Muslim cultures were similarly shaped and influenced by their attachment to the grappling martial arts. In the Indian Subcontinent, the *pehlwan* (wrestler), huddled in the countless *Akharas* dotted across present-day India and Pakistan, is honoured and venerated for his display of strength, impeccable technique and adherence to the way of the Prophet ﷺ.

The grandson of the renowned Indian hadith scholar Shah Waliullah ad-Dihlawi ﷺ, Shah Ismail ﷺ, was known for his proficiency in the Prophetic martial arts and regularly swam over 200km from Dehli to Agra along the Yamuna River.

> ...not content with his literary attainments... He wanted to be a true man of action and acquired high proficiency in all sorts of martial exercises. He was a fine rider, clever marksman, fearless lancer and skilful wrestler.[32]

The Mongolian wrestling form known as Bökh, demands the wearing of boots and a *khuresh*, a cropped cow leather jacket with long sleeves, permitting the gripping of sleeves and collars, whilst

---

31 See Muhammad Manazir Ahsan, *Social Life under the Abbasids*, (SOAS, University of London, 1973).
32 See Abdullah Butt, *Aspects of Shah Ismail Shaheed – Essays on his literary political and religious activities*, (Lahore: Qaum Kutub Khana, 1943).

still holding to a loincloth for the lower garment. Bökh means "durability". Wrestling is the most important of the Mongolian culture's historic "Three Manly Skills", that also include horse-manship and archery. Genghis Khan considered wrestling to be an important way to keep his army in good physical shape and combat-ready.

The court of Qing Dynasty (1646–1911) held regular wrestling events, mainly between ethnic Manchu and Mongol wrestlers. Khuresh, traditional Tuvan jacket wrestling in southern Siberia was influenced by Mongolian wrestling which is evidenced by Khalkha Mongolian and Tuvan wrestlers wearing almost the same jacket. Expressions of modern-day Gulesh wrestling found in Azerbaijan, much like the rest of the Turkic region, seem to adopt more modest combat attire; long shorts with bare chest is the norm.

Communities within the Eastern Chinese Hui people, a perse-cuted Muslim minority, developed highly sophisticated grappling techniques to defend themselves. This was often the fundamental purpose for their uptake of martial arts.

> The association of Hui with martial arts dates to the Yuan period (1279–1368), when Muslims were in the Mongol forces that conquered China. As soldiers in a Mongol army, they would have been familiar with a broad range of martial arts practices, including hand combat, wrestling, archery, and strength training, and they took this orientation with them when they left the military.[33]

The Hui Muslims produced a "number of high-ranking military generals during Qing period" and were particularly active in developing *Shuai-jiao* (Chinese wrestling), which produced a re-nowned twentieth century proponent, Wang Zipang (1881–1973).

---

33 Thomas A. Green, *Martial Arts of the World: An Encyclopedia of History and Innovation, Volume 2,* (ABC-CLIO, 2010), p.343.

In classical Ottoman Oil Wrestling, the importance and almost reverence of the *kispet* (leather wrestling pants made from water buffalo), is considerably unique. Ceremonies would be dedicated to its production and wearing, custom-made for individuals who offer two units of prayer before wearing it, only awarded to wrestlers by merit who possessed courage, discipline, intelligence and refined character.[34] Established "wrestling lodges" or *tekkes* were formed and local wrestling champions would be sponsored by local mosques and given room and board in return for providing wrestling instruction to the community.[35] The celebrated Ottoman explorer, Evliya Çelebi, wrote on the wrestling lodges dotted around the Empire in his landmark 10-volume travelogue, *Seyahatname*,[36] and saw grappling as "an essential of Islam."[37]

The armies of the Ottoman Empire, from the infantry to high-ranking officers and even the Sultans, were well-versed in the grappling arts and combat:

> The Ottoman Empire lived for war. Every governor in this empire was a general; every policeman was a janissary; every mountain pass had its guards, and every road a military destination. The most willowy and doe-eyed pageboy was a dab hand with the gerit or the bow, and well-versed in wrestling, the king of Ottoman sports. At the siege of Baghdad in 1683, when the Persians demanded the contest be decided by single combat, they put up a Herculean warrior from their ranks, and Sultan Mehmet IV took him on himself, splitting the Persian champion's mailed head in two with a single blow.[38]

34 Gul, Turkmen, Dogan & Soyguden, "Lost Tradition in Kirkpinar Oil Wrestling: Importance of Kispet and Ceremony of Kispet Wearing," 2.
35 Thomas A. Green, *Martial Arts of the World: An Encyclopedia of History and Innovation, Volume 2* (ABC-CLIO, 2010).
36 For an English translation of part of this work, see Robert Dankoff & Sooyong Kim, *An Ottoman Traveller: Selections from the Book of Travels by Evliya Çelebi*, (Eland Publishing, 2011).
37 Dever, "Sports Lodges in the Ottoman Empire Depicted in the Travel Book (Seyahat-Name) of Evliya Çelebi," 29.
38 Jason Goodwin, *Lords of the Horizons – A History of the Ottoman Empire* (London: Vintage Books, 2010) p.65.

In recent times, the success of several Muslim MMA fighters originating from the Caucasus—a land of mountainous and rugged terrain—has inspired a new generation. Many attribute their harsh and indefatigable combative style of fighting to the land from which they originate—Dagestan specifically, but the Caucasus more generally. This area has experienced the most ethnopolitical conflict and warfare of any region in the Eurasian continent in recent times. Its disputed borders, diverse nation makeup and conflicted history with the former Soviet Union, coupled with the death and displacement of millions of IDPs (internally displaced persons), has spawned an inherently hardy and resilient generation of people.

> The Caucasus, throughout its history, has been a borderland. It has been an area over which empires competed; an area in which civilisations and religions have met; it has served both as a barrier and bridge to contacts between north and south, east and west. Its crucial geopolitical position—lying between the historical Tsarist, Safavid and Ottoman empires as well as also between regional powers of the twentieth century: Russia, Iran and Turkey—has been a mixed blessing. More often than not, the Caucasian peoples have lost rather than gained from their important geopolitical position...[39]

In the context of grappling, it is sufficient to note that of all the countries, autonomous republics, and federal regions (23 in total) that nominally make up the region between the Black and Caspian Seas, a land with no less than twenty-six distinct ethnicities and an incredibly rich linguistic landscape, all practise and preserve indigenous and hybrid wrestling styles throughout. Over the past century, the dominance of the wrestlers from this region alone in world and Olympic championships across both freestyle and Greco wrestling styles is staggering, outstripping

39 Svante Cornell, *Small Nations and Great Powers – A study of the ethnopolitical conflict in the Caucasus*, (Curzon Press, 2001).

nations with populations three times larger, with most of the medallists—often initially representing neighbouring countries—likewise of Caucasian descent. Whilst some opine that this wrestling culture, similar to how football is played in modern Britain, is used as a means of "controlling the masses" in a deeply volatile region,[40] the grappling nations that make up the Caucasus, the inevitable mettle honed through conflict and the history of grappling amongst the Muslim populace counter such opinions.

---

40 "Fight Club: The wrestlers of Chechnya and Dagestan compete as Russians. But in the hills — and even the gym — Russia is still the enemy," Date accessed August 1 2020, https://olympics.time. com/2012/07/19/olympic-russian-wrestling/

PART II

Martial Warriors Amongst the
Companions ﷺ

وَٱلسَّٰبِقُونَ ٱلْأَوَّلُونَ مِنَ ٱلْمُهَٰجِرِينَ وَٱلْأَنصَارِ وَٱلَّذِينَ ٱتَّبَعُوهُم بِإِحْسَٰنٍ
رَّضِىَ ٱللَّهُ عَنْهُمْ وَرَضُوا۟ عَنْهُ وَأَعَدَّ لَهُمْ جَنَّٰتٍ تَجْرِى تَحْتَهَا ٱلْأَنْهَٰرُ خَٰلِدِينَ
فِيهَآ أَبَدًا ۚ ذَٰلِكَ ٱلْفَوْزُ ٱلْعَظِيمُ ۞ ١٠٠:٩

As for the first and foremost of the Emigrants (*Muhājirīn*)
and the Supporters (*Ansār*) and those who followed them in
goodness, God is pleased with them and they are pleased with
God, and He has prepared for them gardens beneath which
rivers flow, where they will live for ever. That is the
supreme achievement. (Qur'an, 9:100)

Crunch. As ribs collide in a body-to-body takedown on the
hard, sandy makeshift pit within the confines of Medīnah, the
midday heat saps all the energy left in the body. All eyes are on
the pair who have locked horns in the middle, tugging and tus-
sling with exhausting frequency. The sharp grains of sand leave
searing grazes on the elbows and knees as they spar relentlessly.
Wrist grips are exchanged and holds on the back of the neck slip
repeatedly as the sweat drips, landing in concentric patterns on
the desert floor.

The young boys shout loud encouragements as their friends'
strain and grunt with a visible urgency to finish the job. The
seasoned adults look on, intrigued by the unconventional and
often erratic techniques used. The takedown, a seemingly simple

26

concept—putting your opponent's back to the ground as he tries to do the same—can leave the fittest and most able gasping and fatigued to the point they can't continue.

The Prophet Muhammad ﷺ had by this point received a sealed letter from Mecca, sent by his uncle 'Abbās, warning him of an army of three thousand men heading towards Medīnah. By the time the letter was received, the Prophet ﷺ understood that the army had already made considerable progress and following a consultation with his Companions to engage in battle, he readied himself for war.

The Companions ﷺ—now regretting their recommendation to the Prophet ﷺ in taking the fight outside of Medīnah[41]—lined up and looked on in awe and veneration. With his turban wound tightly round his helmet, a breastplate over a coat of mail and a leather sword belt, the Prophet ﷺ appeared in his warrior-best, memorably remarking, "It is not befitting a Prophet once he has put on his armour to take it off until God has judged between him and his enemies."

Marching towards *Shaykhayn*, midway between Medīnah and Uḥud, the Prophet ﷺ led his troops in the Maghrib prayer, after which he reviewed all the soldiers present. Noticing the handful of younger Companions present, he ordered them to return home, to which they protested.

A talented young archer called Rafi' ibn Khadīj ﷺ was permitted to fight, which provoked Samurah ibn Jandub ﷺ, a formidable wrestler, to complain to the Prophet ﷺ that he could throw Rafi'. The Prophet ﷺ instructed the two boys to grapple. It was here, on the cusp of the Battle of Uḥud and under the intense yet watchful gaze of the Prophet ﷺ, that Samurah proved his worth and decisively out-grappled Rafi', taking him down. The other boys were then told to return to their families.

---

41 See Part IV, Narration 10 for a full account.

As varied in temperament, outlook and nature as the Companions of the Messenger of God ﷺ were, they also shared in great combative skills, physical strength and immense courage. Grappling, the staple of every young Arab's martial training, supplemented the other martial abilities of these courageous followers.

ABŪ BAKR

Addressing the people, 'Ali ibn Abī Tālib ؓ, when asked about who displayed the most courage amongst the Companions during the Battle of Badr, said:

> ...the most courageous person is Abū Bakr. We had constructed a shed for RasulAllah ﷺ (during the Battle of Badr) and then asked who would remain with RasulAllah ﷺ so that the Mushrikeen do not attack him. By God! Whenever a Mushrik even drew close to us Abū Bakr was there with his sword drawn near the head side of RasulAllah ﷺ. He attacked anyone who dared attack RasulAllah ﷺ. He was certainly the bravest of people...
>
> By God! None of us dared go close to RasulAllah ﷺ (for fear of being beaten) besides Abū Bakr. *He would hit one person, wrestle with another and shake someone else* as he said, "Shame on you people! Will you kill a man for saying, 'Allah is my Rabb'?"[42]

'UMAR IBN AL-KHATTĀB

Amongst the most capable of the senior Companions was undoubtedly the stellar 'Umar ibn al-Khattāb ؓ. 'Umar had a commanding presence and was not only tall, strong and athletic, but a formidable wrestler and imbued martial conduct. Ambidextrous, 'Umar's reputation as a grappler saw him regularly contest the strong men of Arabia at the renowned Souq al-'Ukāz.

---

42 Muhammad Yusuf Kandhlawi, *Hayatus Sahabah – The Lives of the Sahabah, Vol. 1,* (Islamic Book Service, 2010), p.281.

28

'Umar, whilst known for his just ways and abstemiousness, was respected (and feared) by the leaders of the Quraysh and ultimately, through his conversion, provided reassurance and confidence to the small, early Muslim community. This opened the doors to the public call to Islam. His fearless, imposing nature was no better encapsulated than in the endorsement of the Prophet ﷺ:

> O son of Khattāb, by the one in whose hand is my soul, whenever Satan sees you taking a path, he will only but take another. (Bukhārī)

'ALĪ IBN ABĪ TĀLIB

Upon the revelation of the verse "And warn the nearest people of your clan" (Qur'an, 26:214), the Prophet ﷺ gathered Banu 'Abd al-Muttalib for a meal in the hope of conveying his message to his closest family members.

"O sons of 'Abd al-Muttalib, I know of no Arab who has come to his people with a nobler message than mine. I bring you the best of this world and the next. God has commanded me to call you unto Him. Which of you, then, will help me in this, and be my brother, my executor and my successor amongst you?"

The prolonged silence was broken by the voice of a thirteen-year-old boy, who said, "O Prophet of God, I will be your helper in this." This young boy was to grow in the household of the Prophet ﷺ and later become one of Islam's most exemplary and sagacious warriors; he was 'Alī ibn Abī Tālib ﷺ. 'Ali was born ten years before the first revelation of the Qur'an and delivered inside the Ka'ba.[43] Despite being of average height, he was powerfully built with a large beard. His shoulders were broad, the bones of which are described as the bones of a lion, and "there was no difference between his forearm and upper arm."[44] An impressive soldier and ardent wrestler, he fought valiantly in all the military campaigns

---

43   Dr. Ali. M. Sallabi, 'Ali ibn Abi Talib – Vol. 1, (International Islamic Publishing House, 2011) p.53.
44   Ibid. p.67.

of the Messenger of God ﷺ with the exception of Tabūk. He was married to Fatimah ☙, daughter of the Messenger of God ﷺ, who bore him two sons, Hasan ☙ and Husayn ☙.

On the day of the Battle of Khaybar,[45] the Prophet ﷺ gave ʿAli the standard banner; the honour of carrying the Muslim army flag during battle was one reserved only for the elite amongst the Companions:

> It was narrated from ʿAbd Allāh ibn Ahmed Ibn Hanbal from Jābir that when the Prophet ﷺ gave the standard to Ali ☙, on the day of Khaybar, he quickly said to them, "Join me until we reach the castle," where he tore the castle door from its hinges and off the earth, then seventy men set upon him; he defended himself from them.[46]

HASAN IBN ʿALI

Hasan ☙ was the eldest child of the Prophet's ﷺ daughter Fatimah and ʿAli ibn Abī Tālib, born with the *athan* and *iqama* being recited softly into his ears and named by none other than the Prophet ﷺ himself. As a toddler, he was seen in and around *Masjid an-Nabawi*, playfully climbing upon the Prophet ﷺ during prayer.

> ʿIkrimah Ibn ʿAbbas ☙ said: The Messenger of God ﷺ used to carry al-Hasan on his shoulders. A man once said, "What a blessed mount you are upon, dear child." The Prophet ﷺ said, "What a blessed rider."

HUSAYN IBN ʿALI

His younger brother, Husayn, was born having the blessed saliva of his grandfather ﷺ placed in his mouth and named on the seventh day by him in the month of Shaʿban in the fourth

---

45 The Battle of Khaybar was fought in the year 628 between Muslims and the Jews living in the oasis of Khaybar, located 150 kilometers (93 miles) from Medinah in the north-western part of the Arabian peninsula, in modern-day Saudi Arabia.
46 Ibid. p.159.

year of the migration. Husayn is said to have resembled the Messenger of God 鑭 physically and performed the pilgrimage (*Hajj*) twenty-five times by foot.

Endowed with courage from childhood, both brothers would often be found wrestling in front of the Messenger of God 鑭:

> Hasan 鑭 and Husayn 鑭 were wrestling before the Messenger of God 鑭. The Messenger of God 鑭 was saying, "Come on Hasan." Fatimah asked, "O Messenger of God, why do you say 'Come on Al-Hasan?'" He 鑭 replied, "Gabriel is saying 'Come on Husayn.'"[47]

Nothing is more intense than the sight of sibling rivalry, and nothing endears the heart more than the affection of grandparents.

HAMZA IBN 'ABD AL-MUTTALIB

Another member of the household of the Prophet 鑭 and widely considered one of the greatest wrestlers amongst the Arabs was the paternal uncle of the Prophet 鑭, Hamza ibn 'Abd al-Muttalib.

When Abū Jahl ridiculed his blessed nephew and his message, Hamza 鑭 took it upon himself to take "physical" retribution, fearlessly striking his own uncle with his bow amid all the tribal leaders. This altercation forced Hamza 鑭 to take introspective stock of his otherworldly life and promptly led him to the House of al-Arqam, where he accepted the faith his nephew 鑭 preached. He fought valiantly in the Battle of Badr and killed Utbah ibn Rabi'ah in single combat.

Hamza 鑭 was martyred in the Battle of Uḥud on 3 Shawwal 3AH when he was 59 (lunar) years old. He was standing in front of the Prophet Muhammad 鑭, fighting with two swords and shouting, "I am the Lion of God!"[48]

---

47 See Part IV, Narration 14 of the present work.
48 Muhammad ibn Saad, *Kitab al-Tabaqat al-Kabair*, Vol. 3. Translated by Bewley, A. *The Companions of Badr*, (Ta-Ha Publishers 2013).

Khālid ibn al-Walīd

The grappling abilities of Khālid ibn al-Walīd ﷺ, who was one of the greatest army commanders to have ever lived, are renowned. He served under Abū Bakr ﷺ and 'Umar ibn Khattāb ﷺ. It was under his military leadership that Arabia, for the first time in history, was united under a single political entity, the Caliphate. The Messenger of God ﷺ said "What an excellent slave of God: Khālid ibn Al-Walīd, one of the swords of God, unleashed against the unbelievers!" (Tirmidhī).

His impressive foresight, strategies and victories are studied to this day by Western military institutions, such as the United States Army War College.[49] Khālid's ﷺ grappling skills were established early on in his youth:

> The boys were well-matched. Of about the same age, they were in their early teens. Both were tall and lean, and newly formed muscles rippled on their shoulders and arms as their sweating bodies glistened in the sun. The tall boy was perhaps an inch taller than Khālid. And their faces were so alike that one was often mistaken for the other.
>
> Khālid threw the tall boy; but this was no ordinary fall. As the tall boy fell there was a distinct crack, and a moment later the grotesquely twisted shape of his leg showed that the bone had broken. The stricken boy lay motionless on the ground, and Khālid stared in horror at the broken leg of his friend and nephew. (The tall boy's mother, Hantamah bint Hisham bin al-Mugheerah, was Khālid's first cousin).
>
> In course of time the injury healed and the leg of the tall boy became whole and strong again. He would wrestle again and be among the best of wrestlers. And the two boys would remain friends. But while they were both intelligent, strong and forceful by nature, neither

---

49 Dr Christian Keller, *Intentional Ignorance? – USAWC, PME, and Middle Eastern Theory and History*, (Strategy research paper by USAWC, 2016).

had patience or tact. They were to continue to compete with each other in almost everything that they did.

The reader should make a mental note of this tall boy, for he was to play an important role in the life of Khālid. He was the son of Al-Khaṭṭāb and his name was ʿUmar.[50]

Rukānah ibn Abī Yazīd

In understanding and uncovering the grappling prowess of the Messenger of God ﷺ, we are indebted to the legendary strong man of Arabia, Rukānah ibn Abī Yazīd ﷺ. A capable man yet only conversant in the "physical", he was defeated emphatically by the Messenger of God ﷺ on several occasions. His personal account in the annals of Islamic martial history provides an insight into a noble man humbling himself, able to embrace and see divine truth through the "war of attrition" that played out between him and the Messenger of God ﷺ. He died in 42AH during the reign of Muʿāwiyah ﷺ.

Samurah ibn Jundub

Samurah ibn Jundub ﷺ was considered amongst the most brave and noble youth of the Companions belonging to the Ghatafan tribe. In keeping with the normative traits of young men at the time, who from "an early age were taught to ride, wield a sword, use a bow, travel hard and sleep rough, finding their food where they could", Samurah's tremendous grappling skills convinced the Messenger of God ﷺ to allow him to fight at Uḥud. He fought in later campaigns and died in 59AH in Basra, Iraq.

---

50 A.I. Akram, *Sword of Allāh – Khalid bin al-Waleed*, (Maktabah Publishers & Distributors, 2004), p.1.

Women Warriors

Contrary to stereotypical assumptions, it may surprise many that some of the most notable martial artists among the Companions of the Prophet 鬱 were women. The role of Muslim women during military campaigns was mainly to nurse the sick and injured, retrieve weaponry and armaments, and to mind property and children. Umayya bint Qays ibn ʿAbīʾs as-Salt al Ghifārīyya 鬱 recalls how she and the women of her tribe, Banu Ghifār, wished to treat the wounded at the Battle of Khaybar, to which the Prophet 鬱 agreed and as a young girl, placed her on the back saddle of his camel en route to the battle.[51]

Many women, specifically in the case of the Quraysh, were strategically "deployed" as sensual distractions or to attract sympathy from opposing forces. What is clear from the numerous accounts relating to women's bravery and combat in battle, was

---

51 Muhammad Ibn Sad's *Kitab at-Tabaqat al-Kabir, Vol.8 – The Women of Madina* (Ta-Ha Publishers Ltd, 1995), p.204. Umayya bint Qays' encounter with the Prophet 鬱 illustrates his humanity, mercy, and clement nature. As a young girl, she desired to help at the Battle of Khaybar. Upon requesting that she and the other women join the men at Khaybar to tend to the wounded, the Prophet 鬱 approved and placed her on the back saddle of the camel. When the camel halted en route, she noticed traces of blood running down the side of the animal. Embarrassed, she clung to the camel and waited. Upon seeing Umayya, the Messenger of God 鬱 said, "Perhaps you have menstruated?" and suggested that she discreetly take a water vessel and tend to herself using salt in the water as a cleansing agent to wash the blood. After the Muslims had conquered Khaybar, she recalls how the Messenger of God 鬱 had gifted her a necklace, placing it upon her with his blessed hands. The necklace remained on her until she died, saying "By God, it will never leave me." She left instructions that she be buried with the necklace and her body washed with salted water. May God be well pleased with her.

the general acceptability amongst the Muslims for women to engage in martial arts and indeed fight when necessary, but also their own desire to learn and participate, with many of the female Companions being forthright and deeply courageous. In fact, in Ibn Sa'd's *al-Tabaqat*, in a volume entirely dedicated to "The Women of Medīnah", there is not a single rebuke on the part of the Prophet 鑶 against women and their martial conduct. Far from the dismissive distortions one reads in modern media, the following lend plentiful examples for the pursuit of martial training and a healthy physical culture amongst Muslim women.

We read of the likes of Asma bint Abū Bakr 鑶 who fought at the Battle of Yarmūk against a pressing Roman army under the banner of her blessed father, Abū Bakr, in 13AH. She was also known to carry a dagger on her person in self-defence against the thieves of Medīnah, as theft was rife at the time.[52]

Khawlah bint al-Azwār

The renowned traditionist and historian, Al Wāqidī, docu-ments[53] an impressive account of a "mysterious warrior" seen advancing ahead of Khālid ibn al-Walīd 鑶 and his army towards the Roman encampment to rescue the captured Companion Dirar following the Siege of Damascus in 13AH (634CE) under the Caliphate of Abū Bakr 鑶.

Khālid's veteran eyes noticed "the rider's behaviour and ap-pearance projected a kind of wisdom and the riding-style showed bravery."

> The mysterious warrior pounced on the enemy like a mighty hawk on a tiny sparrow in an attack that wreaked havoc in the Roman lines and by perpetrating a massacre penetrated to their very centre. It was like lightning striking the head of two or four youths, then burning to ashes another five or seven and then flashing

---

52 Ibid, p.179.
53 The ascription of *Futuh as-Sham* to al-Wāqidī is disputed; however, the attribution of these works to him should be taken simply as indicative of his renown as a historian of the early period.

yet again. Reaching the centre, the warrior displayed clear signs of frustration and anxiety and then began attacking again, ripping the Christian lines apart and advancing until the Muslims lost sight of this champion who all the while was growing ever more anxious.[54]

Many of the Muslim soldiers mistook the rider as Khālid, until he himself arrived moments later. Khālid and his men aligned in rank order, poised to join the fight, when again the lone rider singlehandedly attacked several Romans at one time. When they finally rallied the rider into the Muslim lines, Khālid's numerous requests to uncover the identity of this warrior was met with silence. The Muslim cavalry pressed further until finally a feminine voice replied,

> O Commander, I have not avoided you out of disobedience, but out of modesty for I am of those who seclude themselves behind the veil. My sorrow and broken heart forced me here.

It was none other than Dirar's sister, the legendary Khawlah bint al-Azwār ﷺ. Khawlah was a woman of martial combat, brave and strategic, who fought alongside Khālid ibn al-Walīd in several battles in Syria, Jordan and Palestine. Descending from the tribe of Assad, her family were amongst the earliest converts to Islam and could be described as something of a martial family, with her brother Dirar himself a leading general under Khālid ibn al-Walīd. Khawlah ﷺ was an unrivalled swordswoman, adept in riding, archery and spear play, and fought in the battle of Sanīta al-'Uqab and Ajnadayn.

ṢAFIYYAH BINT ʿABD AL-MUTTALIB

The courage displayed by the *Sahābiyyat* ﷺ, in the face of certain death, was indicative of disciplined practice and ingrained readiness. Often surpassing the men, we see in the example of Ṣafiyyah bint ʿAbd al-Muttalib ﷺ—the beloved aunt of the

54 Al-Imam al-Waqidi, *The Islamic Conquest of Syria*, (Ta-Ha Publishers Ltd, 2009), p.75.

Messenger of God ﷺ, a strikingly bold woman who at the Battle of Uḥud—upon seeing the Muslims flee and the reneging of the only male presence, Hassan ibn Thabit—assassinated a Jewish intruder in South-East Medīnah in an act of self-defence by use of a club.[55] She was also known for the stern way she reared her son, Zubayr ibn al-'Awwām. She physically disciplined him as a child in hope of making him a strong and capable man, to the extent that as a young boy he fought with a man so fiercely that he broke the man's hand. Pregnant at the time, Ṣafiyyah even carried the man home out of compassion and when onlookers asked what had happened, she replied, "He fought al-Zubayr. Did you find al-Zubayr soft like cheese or dates or full of brass?"[56]

NUSAYBAH BINT KA'B

We cannot fail to mention the great Nusaybah bint Ka'b ﷺ, a woman of the Ansār and one of the two women to have sworn an oath of allegiance to the Messenger of God ﷺ directly at the second pledge of Aqabah. She was an outspoken, ambitious and truly brave woman, to whom God responded when she asked the Prophet ﷺ why God only addressed men and not women in the Qur'an, with the beautiful verses of Sūrah Ahzab:

إِنَّ ٱلْمُسْلِمِينَ وَٱلْمُسْلِمَاتِ وَٱلْمُؤْمِنِينَ وَٱلْمُؤْمِنَاتِ وَٱلْقَانِتِينَ وَٱلْقَانِتَاتِ وَٱلصَّادِقِينَ وَٱلصَّادِقَاتِ وَٱلصَّابِرِينَ وَٱلصَّابِرَاتِ وَٱلْخَاشِعِينَ وَٱلْخَاشِعَاتِ وَٱلْمُتَصَدِّقِينَ وَٱلْمُتَصَدِّقَاتِ وَٱلصَّائِمِينَ وَٱلصَّائِمَاتِ وَٱلْحَافِظِينَ فُرُوجَهُمْ وَٱلْحَافِظَاتِ وَٱلذَّاكِرِينَ ٱللَّهَ كَثِيرًا وَٱلذَّاكِرَاتِ أَعَدَّ ٱللَّهُ لَهُم مَّغْفِرَةً وَأَجْرًا عَظِيمًا ۝ ٣٣:٣٥

55 Muhammad ibn Saad, *Kitab at-Tabaqat al-Kabir, Vol.8: The Women of Madina* (Ta-Ha Publishers Ltd, 1995).
56 Muhammad ibn Saad, *Kitab al-Tabaqat al-Kabir, Vol.3: The Companions of Badr* (Ta-Ha Publishers Ltd, 2013)

For men and women who are devoted to God—believing
men and women, obedient men and women, truthful men
and women, steadfast men and women, humble men and
women, charitable men and women, fasting men and women,
chaste men and women, men and women who remember
God often—God has prepared forgiveness and a rich reward.
(Qur'an, 33:35)

A renowned martial artist from amongst the Companions,
Nusaybah ﷺ was distinguished by her courage in defending the
Messenger of God ﷺ at the Battle of Uḥud. Her initial role was to
deliver water to the soldiers and tend to the wounded. However,
upon seeing the archers disobey the command of the Prophet
ﷺ and leave their posts, causing the battle to sway against the
Muslims, Nusaybah ﷺ unsheathed her sword and rushed to
defend the Prophet ﷺ, to which he testified: "Wherever I turned,
left or right on the day of Uḥud, I saw her fighting for me."

She was afflicted by thirteen wounds on the day of Uḥud, at
the end of which the Prophet ﷺ saw her, and called to her son,
"Your mother! Your mother! See to her wounds, may God bless
you and your household! Your mother has fought better than so-
and-so." When Nusaybah ﷺ heard what the Prophet ﷺ said, she
said, "Pray to God that we may accompany you in Paradise." He
ﷺ said, "O God, make them my companions in Paradise." She
participated in the battles of Uḥud, Hunāin, Khaybar, Yamāmah
and the Treaty of Hudaybiyyah.

Bodyguards of the Messenger

From the most formidable combatants among the Companions were undoubtedly those chosen to serve as personal bodyguards of the Messenger of God 灠, inside and outside of battle. This was until the revelation "God will protect you from the people",[57] upon which he 灠 no longer permitted anyone to guard him. Prophetic chroniclers list the following from amongst them:

SA'D IBN ABĪ WAQQĀS

Sa'd ibn Abī Waqqās 灠 was from the outset a forthright and courageous man. He was one of the earliest to convert to Islam through Abū Bakr 灠 and honoured as being from amongst the Ten Elect Companions given the promise of paradisial entry in this life by the Prophet 灠 himself. He fought in all the Prophetic campaigns and was the renowned master archer of the Companions, known for having his supplications readily answered, releasing the first arrow for the sake of Islam and firing a thousand arrows at the Battle of Uḥud. Under the caliphate of 'Umar ibn al-Khaṭṭāb, Sa'd become governor of Kūfah and led the armies in the Battle of Qādissiyyah against the Persians in which thirty thousand Muslim soldiers faced a battalion of

57 Qur'an, 5:67.

a hundred thousand. He was the last of the Emigrants to pass, died in Medīnah and was buried in al-Baqi'.

Sa'd ibn Ubāda

He is Sa'd ibn 'Ubāda ibn Dulaym, chief of the Sā'ida clan of the Khazraj in Medīnah. He accepted Islam prior to the Hijra, thus is of the Ansār and a prominent Companion of the Messenger of God ﷺ. He was considered a "perfect" Arab due to his mastery of archery, ability to swim and proficiency in reading and writing the Arabic language. Sa'd was a celebrated soldier and participated in the campaigns of Uḥud, Dumat al-Jandal, Khandaq, Muraysi, Khaybar and the Conquest of Mecca, Hunāyn and Tāif. He died some five years after the passing of the Messenger of God ﷺ.

Sa'd ibn Mu'adh

Sa'd ibn Mu'ādh ibn al-Nu'mān was chief of the Aws tribe and of the Ansār of Medīnah. He accepted Islam at the hands of Mus'ab ibn 'Umayr, which led to the immediate conversion of the entire Aws tribe. He was a formidable warrior who, on the eve of the Battle of Badr, reassured the Prophet ﷺ by saying:

> By He Who has sent you with the Truth! Never think that we will leave you to fight alone, if it is even out of bonds. And I take an oath with you as the head of the Ansār, you give us what you want, you collect from us what we have. You take us anywhere you want, you push us in any battle, we will defend you, defend till our last breath. No arrow can touch you, until it passes through our chests. We have tied a relationship of life and death with you. If you seek to cross the seas or go in it, we will follow your command and none among us will remain behind. We are patient in war, vicious in battle. May God allow you to witness from our efforts what comforts your eyes. Therefore, march forward with the blessing of God.

He is one of a few Companions to remain on the battlefield at Uḥud when Khālid ibn al-Walīd led the counterattack. He participated in the Battle of Khandaq where he was afflicted with serious wounds, and as a result died shortly after. It is reported in al-Bukhāri that the Messenger of God ﷺ said "The Throne (of God) shook at the death of Saʿd ibn Muʿādh."

MUHAMMAD IBN MASLAMA

Muhammad ibn Maslama, known as "The Knight of God's Prophet",[58] was born twenty-two years prior to Prophethood. He was from the Ansār and one of few to be named Muhammad in the Days of Ignorance. He was tall in stature and extremely dark in complexion. He fought in all the wars alongside the Prophet ﷺ except Tabūk as he was asked by the Prophet ﷺ to govern Medīnah while he was away in battle. He was put in charge of fifty men tasked with patrolling the Muslim camp on the night of the Battle of Uḥud and was later seen as one of few who stood by the Prophet ﷺ when the majority retreated.

The Prophet ﷺ sent Muhammad ibn Maslama with ten other Companions on an expedition to Dhul Qaṣṣa, where they arrived at nightfall. Whilst asleep at their campsite, they were surrounded by one hundred men who unleashed a barrage of arrows upon them. Ibn Maslama jumped up from his sleep to fire back upon the attackers, but all ten of the Companions were murdered, leaving Ibn Maslama as the lone survivor of the onslaught. In later years which saw great division amongst senior Companions, Muhammad ibn Maslama was considered one of four that was safe from tribulation (*Fitna*) due to the explicit instructions given to him by the Messenger of God.[59] He died at the age of 77.

---

58 Muhammad ibn Saad. *Kitab al-Tabaqat al-Kabir, Vol. 3: The Companions of Badr,* (Ta-Ha Publishers Ltd, 2013).
59 Fuad Jabali, *The Companions of the Prophet – A Study of Geographical Distribution and Political Arguments,* (Brill, 2003).

ZUBAYR IBN AL-'AWWĀM

Zubayr ibn al-'Awwām was the son of Ṣafiyyah bint 'Abd al-Muttalib and thus the first paternal cousin of the Messenger of God ﷺ. From a young age, he was renowned for his disciplined upbringing and martial capabilities. He regularly answered the call for single combat in the lead up to battles, which saw him defeat his opponents with ease. The Prophet ﷺ said "Indeed for every Prophet is a disciple, Al-Zubayr is my disciple." He embraced Islam at a young age and was one of ten promised paradise in this life. Physically, he was dark in complexion, extremely tall and slender, and known to wear a yellow turban replicating the angels who assisted at the Battle of Badr. He passed away in 36AH.

ABŪ AYYŪB AL-ANSĀRI

Abū Ayyūb Khālid ibn Zayd ibn Kulayb ibn Tha'labah al-Ansāri was the first to host the Prophet ﷺ in his own home in Medīnah after he left Mecca, where approximately 180 people miraculously ate from the meals prepared solely for the Prophet and Abū Bakr ﷺ. The Prophet ﷺ remained at the house of Abū Ayyub until *Masjid an-Nabawi* and his own houses were built. Leading a distinguished career as a military leader, Abū Ayyub fought in all the wars of Prophethood and "...did not stay away from any battle in which the Muslims engaged from the time of Muhammad ﷺ to the time of Mu'āwiyah, unless he was at the same time, engaged in another battle being fought elsewhere."[60]

The Messenger of God ﷺ prayed, "O God, stand guard over Abū Ayyub, just as he spent the night standing over me."[61]

'UKĀSHAH IBN MIHṢAN

'Ukāshah was from amongst the early converts to Islam who migrated to Medīnah. A swordsman par excellence, upon

---

60 Muhammad ibn Saad, *Kitab al-Tabaqat al-Kabir, Vol.3: The Companions of Badr*, (Ta-Ha Publishers Ltd, 2013).
61 Ibn Sayyid'n Nās, *Light of the Eyes – An Abridgement of the Biography of the Trusted, The Trustworthy*, translated by Ibrahim Osi-Efa, (Furthest Boundary Press, 2020).

breaking his sword at the Battle of Badr, was famously given a wooden rod by the Messenger of God ﷺ which miraculously transformed into a steel blade in the midst of battle. This sword remained and was used by 'Ukāshah in subsequent wars. He was killed at Buzagha during the reign of Abū Bakr ؓ in the eleventh year after migration.

PART III

Objectives of Sports in Islam

In an inspiring public lecture held in Mecca in 1999, Shaykh Muhammad ibn ʿAlawi al-Mālikī (God have mercy on him)[62] discussed the role of physical exercise in Islam and its associated higher purposes. This was later rendered into a short book titled *Silat al-Riyādati bil-Dīn wa-Dawruha fi Tanshiʾati al-Shabāb al-Muslim* – *The Relation between Exercise and Religion and its Role in the Development of Muslim Youth*, part of which is summarised below:

> The religion of Islam has higher goals and the Divine Law (*Sharīʿa*) of Islam has deeper purposes:
>
> 1. At the head of the list is the pleasure of God. This is the highest goal for the knowers of God.
> 2. The establishment of the Divine Law.
> 3. Spreading of this way (*Dīn*).
> 4. Striving in the path of God.
>
> Abū Hurayrah ﷺ reported: I heard the Messenger of God ﷺ saying, "He who is afraid of the pillage of the

62 Sayyid Muhammad ibn Alawi al-Maliki al-Hasani, born in 1367AH/1944CE in Mecca, was a leading traditional Islamic scholar raised in a household of great learning and scholarship. A major contemporary scholar of hadith, Quranic exegesis, law, doctrine, Prophetic biography and spirituality, he obtained a PhD in Hadith sciences with distinction from al-Azhar University, Egypt when he was twenty-five years old. Like both his father and grandfather who were imams and preachers of the Sacred mosque in Mecca, Sayyid Muhammad would hold regular public teaching sessions in the Sacred Sanctuary, he achieved worldwide recognition and was deeply respected and loved by Muslim scholars everywhere. He travelled extensively, lecturing and attending religious gatherings, visiting Syria, Morocco and Egypt regularly. He made several trips to Malaysia, Singapore, Indonesia, the Yemen and East Africa, and travelled to Pakistan, South Africa, all over Europe and North America. He authored over a hundred works extensively covering a variety of religious, legal, social and historical topics. He passed in the month of Ramadhān in 1424AH/2004CE, with thousands attending his funeral from all over the Muslim world and is buried in the Maʿlā cemetery in Mecca. God have mercy on him.

enemy, sets out in the early part of the night; and he who sets out early, reaches his destination. Be on your guard that the commodity of God is precious. Verily the commodity of God is paradise". (Tirmidhi).

Abū Sa'id Al-Khudri 🙏 said: The Messenger of God 🙏 said, "God, the Lord of honour and glory, will say to the inhabitants of Paradise: 'O inhabitants of Paradise!' They will respond: 'Here we are! At Your service, O our Lord. All good is in Your Hand!' He will ask them: 'Are you pleased?' They will reply: 'Why should we not be pleased, O Lord, when You have given us what You have not given to any of Your creatures?' God will say: 'Shall I not give you something better than that?' They will ask: 'O Lord! What can be better than that?' God will say: 'I shall bestow My Pleasure upon you, and I shall never be displeased with you.'" (Bukhāri and Muslim).

This contentment in the last two hadiths is the ultimate goal and highest purpose that enlightened souls can aim for. The means to reach such goals carries the same ruling as the ultimate goals, provided the means are praiseworthy. An example is fighting for the sake of God's contentment as opposed to emotion or sectarianism. Abū Musa Al-Ash'ari 🙏 reported that the Messenger of God 🙏 was asked about the one who fights in the battlefield out of valour, or out of zeal, or out of hypocrisy, which of these are considered as fighting in the cause of God? He 🙏 said, "He who fights in order that the Word of God remains supreme, is considered as fighting in the cause of God." (Bukhāri and Muslim).

Islam takes the normalities of life, habits, and mundane customs, and aligns them to higher directions. These means are also corrected and refined to be applicable for the service of the Truth, and man is rewarded for them as he would be rewarded for the higher goals. This is not the same as the philosophy of "the ends justify the means". Not all means that take you to praiseworthy destinations, are praiseworthy. Instead, the means that accomplish praiseworthy aims must be sanctioned via revelation or at least not be prohibited. Then, they will become praiseworthy. For actions to be rewarded for their goals, they must be:

1. Aligned towards a higher purpose.
2. Be permissible in and of themselves.

The Relation between Religion and Sports

Sports are means, they are not usually objectives in and of themselves. Provided they are being utilised for a higher objective, they will be praiseworthy. At the advent of Islam, the Arabs had many valuable gifts and skills; however, these were not being utilised for goodness and were wasted. Courage became partisanship, generosity became wastefulness and chivalry was for tribal loyalties only.

Islam nurtured these gifts and gave them a heavenly direction, thus becoming a means for Divine reward. This made it easier for the Arabs to accept because it made use of what they already had. Chivalry and dignity (*ghayrah*) became used for the protection of the family, the religion and the symbols of God; it was thus chivalry in the path of God.

Courage and strength were wasted on destructive wars and bloodshed. Islam turned it towards elevating the word of God. Generosity was turned towards higher goals. Abū Hurayrah reported: The Prophet said, "He who believes in God and the Last Day, let him show hospitality to his guest; and he who believes in God and the Last Day, let him maintain good relation with kin; and he who believes in God and the Last Day, let him speak good or remain silent." (Bukhāri and Muslim).

Narrated by Al-Mughira : Sa`d ibn Ubada said, "If I found a man with my wife, I would kill him with the sharp side of my sword." When the Prophet heard that he said, "Do you wonder at Sa`d's sense of dignity? Verily, I have more sense of dignity than Sa`d, and God has more sense of dignity than I." (Bukhāri).

Natural human inclinations, desires and protective-ness were maintained and turned to the path of God, bestowing martyrdom on the one killed in self-defence. Sa'id ibn Zayd reported: The Prophet ﷺ said, "Whoever is killed protecting his property is a martyr. Whoever is killed protecting his religion is a martyr. Whoever is killed protecting his life is a martyr. Whoever is killed protecting his family is a martyr." (Tirmidhi).

This allows the self to be trained, controlled, and focused towards a higher rank, accruing the benefits of:

1. Contentment of God.
2. The fulfilment of human needs.
3. The fulfilment of human desires.

In conclusion, many of the human attributes that were present among the Arabs were cultivated and turned towards good and made into pathways for higher goals. This coloured them in the dye of the Divine Law.

Many of the physical customs, like modern sports, were present among the Arabs. For example: horseracing, duelling, wrestling, foot racing, archery and swimming. These improve physical qualities, reflexive movements and physical strength that facilitates intellectual rigour. "The strong believer is better and more beloved to God than the weak believer, while there is (still) goodness in both." (Muslim) .

The weak Muslim has belief for himself and weakness for others whereas the strong believer is strong for himself and others. Islam affirms many of the sporting habits of the Arabs, not because they are goals in and of themselves, but because the greater purpose of this faith—to populate the earth with the worship of God alone—can only be attained through strength.

They are means and forms of relaxation because the heart tires and bores of monotony and repetition, as per the statement of Ali ibn Abī Tālib ﵁: "Leave these hearts, for they tire like the bodies tire" (Manawai in Fathul Qadeer, 40:4). And this statement narrated by

Anas ibn Mālik 🙵: "Give the hearts rest from time to time" (Musnadul Firdaws, 3181).

Relaxation takes multiple forms: Spiritual— the remembrance of God and recitation of Qur'an, Intellectual—reading poetry and literature. This includes strengthening one's willpower and manifesting physical strength in Islam. It revives a person and makes him anew, with a fresh will and activeness. Abū Darda 🙵 says: "Indeed, I leave my heart to some trivialities (permissible distractions) to reinvigorate me for the Truth" (Manawi, Fathul Qadeer, 40:4).

Islam came with the truth, guidance, light, goodness, knowledge and felicity. Spiritual struggle and combative engagement (Jihād) were mandated to spread this goodness and to teach it to the people; to destroy falsehood and to command good and forbid evil. So, many skills were promoted that would facilitate these meanings and guarantee these goals. People were encouraged and called to them, and love for them was ingrained in their hearts. Rewards and heavenly felicity were attached to them and many magnificent blessings—of this world and the next, physical and spiritual. This made mundane custom, religious ritual and worship delightful and enjoyable. Obedience was relaxing and turning to God was done happily and with delight. It was for this reason that rushing to and competing in these arenas of goodness was witnessed. No other nation has this level of historical testimony, praising and honouring its accomplishments in these fields.

Over twenty years ago, a short article called *Sport and Islam*[63] penned by Shaykh Muhammad's student, Shaykh Seraj Hendricks[64]

63 Seraj Hendricks, "Sport and Islam," Muslim Views, Date accessed August 1 2020, http://mysite. mweb.co.za/residents/mfj1/sport.htm
64 Sheikh Seraj Hasan Hendricks was an internationally recognised leading Islamic scholar who was appointed khalīfa of the distinguished al-Sayyid Muhammad b. ʿAlawī al-Mālikī. He was Resident Sheikh of Azzawia Institute in Cape Town, and holder of the Maqasid Chair at the International Peace University of South Africa. He was previously head of the Muslim Judicial Council's Fatwa Committee (which often led to him being described as the "Mufti of Cape Town"), lecturer in fiqh at

(God have mercy upon him), a classically educated South African scholar, confirmed what was previously the hallmark of well-rounded and wholesome believers. In an age of inane lifelong obsessions with spectator sports, an insatiable adrenal thirst for the highest, fastest, most extreme games we can concoct, this article succinctly identifies the primary—and clearly the more sacred—objectives of sports in the context of the Islamic tradition and presumably summarises the above text.

More recently, in the custom of the great traditionalists (*muhaddithūn*) of the past, a compilation of forty ahadith on the sports of the Messenger of God ﷺ by Shaykh Muhammad Khayr Ramadan Yusuf was published in Arabic,[65] providing a much-needed revival of the importance of permitted sports, physical training and martial arts.

It is unfortunate how little has been written on the martial and physical activities of the great Muslims of the past. It is as though the daily physical engagement of horse riding, hunter gathering of provision, firewood and the martial training needed to perpetually fend off aggressors was simply a given and barely needed mentioning. Despite the encouraging example and words of the Messenger of God ﷺ, modern lifestyles seem to have blinded most Muslims, leaving them with a misgiven and shallow view of the martial way.

There is an undoubted importance in practising the established ritual forms of worship, embedded in the communal and social obligations Islam advocates. A lifelong commitment to learning and fulfilment of the Sacred Law in all its permutations is similarly required. Yet, the physical endeavours of this religion's noble founder ﷺ are often overlooked. We just don't give the

the Islamic College of Southern Africa (ICOSA), and lecturer in the Study of Islam at the University of Johannesburg (UJ). He was a member of the Stanlib Sharī'a Board, and chief arbitrator (Hakīm) of the Crescent Observer's Society. Sheikh Seraj was actively engaged in the anti-apartheid struggle in South Africa during the 80s and early 90s. Nominated as one of the world's most influential Muslims by *The Muslim 500*. He passed away in Ramadhān 1442AH/July 2020. God have mercy on him.
65 See Muhammad Khayr Ramadan Yusuf's *Al-'Arbaun al-Riyadha – Forty Ahadith on the Virtues of Sports* (Dar Tayyiba L'Nashr wa Tawzee', 1425AH/ 2004). This work is currently being translated into English and is due to be published.

physical activity of the Prophet ﷺ the same value as other acts of worship; or worse, we don't see it as worship at all.

Comparing the Righteous Companions ﷺ of the Prophet ﷺ by today's standards, would liken them to super athletes. The context within which they lived preserved their lives, fed their young, cultured their sustenance and led them to prevail in the harsh and unforgiving deserts of Arabia. Admittedly, to the best of the author's knowledge, the precise details of constitution, structure and rules applied by the Messenger of God ﷺ and his Companions and their practice of grappling has not been fully documented. However, what is established and arguably of greater import are the principal objectives of practising the martial arts of the Prophet ﷺ.

Broadly gathered from the limited literature in English on what can be considered as the objectives of participating in sport in Islam, there appears to be a consensus on the following.

Military Function

وَأَعِدُّواْ لَهُم مَّا ٱسْتَطَعْتُم مِّن قُوَّةٍ وَمِن رِّبَاطِ ٱلْخَيْلِ تُرْهِبُونَ بِهِۦ عَدُوَّ ٱللَّهِ وَعَدُوَّكُمْ وَءَاخَرِينَ مِن دُونِهِمْ لَا تَعْلَمُونَهُمُ ٱللَّهُ يَعْلَمُهُمْ ۚ وَمَا تُنفِقُواْ مِن شَىْءٍ فِى سَبِيلِ ٱللَّهِ يُوَفَّ إِلَيْكُمْ وَأَنتُمْ لَا تُظْلَمُونَ ۝ ٦٠:٨

And prepare against them whatever you are able of strength
and of horses tethered by which you may terrify the enemy of
God and your enemy and others besides them whom you do
not know [but] whom God knows. And whatever you spend
in the cause of God will be fully repaid to you, and you will
not be wronged. (Qur'an, 8:60)

The art of war teaches us to rely not on the likelihood
of the enemy's not coming, but on our own readiness to
receive him. (Sun Tzu)[66]

It is noteworthy that the Messenger of God ﷺ engaged in a
total of twenty-nine military expeditions in his blessed lifetime,
of which actual fighting occurred in only eleven, with less than
1,700 casualties on both sides.[67]

---

66 Sun Tzu, *Sun Tzu on the Art of War*, translated by Lionel Giles, (Allandale Online Publishing, 2000), p.31.
67 *The Biography of the Prophet Muhammad – Abridged* (Deen Intensive 2012).

53

The Arabian Peninsula was "conquered at a cost of less than 250 men killed on the battlefields, on the enemy side. Loss of Muslims was at the rate of one martyr a month for a period of ten years at an average. This respect of human blood is unequalled in the annals of man."[68]

The primacy of wrestling—we could include all grappling arts by extension—as a mode of martial combat suitable for military participation is established through the Messenger of God ﷺ in Narration 11 of Imam Suyūṭī's *Al-Musār'ah ilā al-Muṣār'ah*, located in Part IV of the present work.

> On the authority of Samurah ibn Jundub ؓ: The Prophet ﷺ would inspect the young men of Anṣār every year. Whoever amongst them attained maturity, he ﷺ would accept for military service. During an inspection one year, a young man passed by him ﷺ and he ﷺ sent him to join the army. Then Samurah was assessed by him ﷺ thereafter but was rejected. Samurah thus said, "O Messenger of God ﷺ, you permitted a young man but rejected me, whereas if he was to wrestle me I would defeat him." He ﷺ said, "Go and wrestle him." He said, "So I took him down. He ﷺ thus permitted me to join the army."[69]

The chapter of the Qur'an, Sūrah al-Anfāl "The Spoils", a chapter primarily considered Medinan, of which a major theme relates to the Battle of Badr, was fought about a year after the migration of the Prophet ﷺ from Mecca to Medīnah. It was the first military campaign between the Muslim community and the Quraysh of Mecca whose hostility towards the Muslims continued even after the migration.

Verse 60 states, "And prepare against them whatever you are able of strength ..." which, according to many commentators, was in reference to weapons of war, specifically the archers. However,

---

68 Dr. Muhammad Hamidullah, *The Battlefields of the Prophet Muhammad*, 4th Edition, (Kitab Bhavan, 1992).
69 al-Tabarāni, Mu'jam al Kabīr, al-Hākim – Mustadrak.

a broader understanding of the term "strength"—particularly in the context of warfare—would clearly not discount combative strong men and women.

عَـنْ أَبِـي هُـرَيْـرَةَ رَضِيَ اللهُ تَـعَالَى عَـنْـهُ، قَالَ: قَالَ رَسُولُ اللهِ صَلَّى اللهُ عَـلَـيْهِ وَسَـلَّمَ: «الْـمُؤْمِنُ الْـقَوِيُّ خَـيْـرٌ وَأَحَبُّ إِلَى اللهِ مِنَ الْـمُؤْمِنِ الضَّعِـيْفِ، وَفِي كُلِّ خَيْرٌ. اِحْرِصْ عَـلَى مَا يَـنْـفَـعُـكَ، وَاسْـتَـعِنْ بِاللهِ، وَلَا تَعْجَزْ، وَإِنْ أَصَابَـكَ شَيْءٌ فَلَا تَـقُلْ «لَوْ أَنِّي فَـعَـلْتُ كَـذَا وَكَـذَا»، وَلَـكِنْ قُـلْ: «قَدَّرَ اللهُ وَمَا شَاءَ فَعَلَ»، فَإِنَّ «لَوْ» تَـفْـتَحُ عَمَلَ الشَّـيْطَانِ.

Abū Hurayrah ﷺ reported: The Messenger of God ﷺ said, The strong believer is more beloved to God than the weak believer, but there is goodness in both of them. Be eager for what benefits you, seek help from God, and do not be frustrated. If something befalls you, then do not say: If only I had done something else. Rather say: God has decreed what He wills. Verily, the phrase "if only" opens the way for the work of Satan.[70]

The scholars of hadith have discussed at length what is meant in the above narration with regards to strength. The word "strength" in this Prophetic statement, like many others, is multi-faceted. It can refer to physical strength, both in terms of sickness and ill health, but also in terms of physical fitness to serve the religion (physical combat or manual labour). Amongst the Quraysh was one Abū al-Aswad al-Jumahi, a man so strong that he would stand on a cowhide, and ten men would pull the hide to take it from under his feet, but in the end, the hide would

---

70 Sahih Muslim, 2664.

tear without him having moved an inch. Yet the Prophet ﷺ threw down Abū al-Aswad al-Jumahi with ease, proving his strength was unrivalled.

Another understanding derived from this hadith is with regards to one's courage in propagating truth, as mentioned by the renowned scholar of the 13ᵗʰ century, Ibn Qayyim al-Jawziyya ﷺ,

> The one who has insight into the Truth and an awareness of it, but he is weak and has no strength to implement it or to call to it, then this is the situation of the weak believer. The strong believer is better and more beloved to God than him.[71]

Ibn Qayyim ﷺ also mentioned,

> This hadith does not nullify the strength and courage of one who wrestles other men but instead, it necessitates that the one who controls himself at the time of anger has more right to the title (of strength and courage).[72]

The great Egyptian scholar of the 9ᵗʰ century, Abd al-Wahhāb Ash-Sha'rāni ﷺ stated,

> The main covenant was taken with the Messenger of God ﷺ that we would not become heedless through neglecting to learn the martial arts, such as archery, racing, self-defence and the like. Thereafter that we would not abandon them after having taught (the aforementioned), so that we would not lose our mastery in that regard. Few pay proper attention to this covenant.[73]

This objective of military function eventually spawned the conceptualization of what later became known as *Furusiyya*, a training programme (narrowly translated as "Equitation"), for which a significant amount of scholarship and development was dedicated and eventually led to a rich literary production

71 Ibn al-Qayyim al Jawziyya, *Ad-Dā' Wad-Dawā' - Spiritual Disease and Its Cure* (Al-Firdous Ltd, 2006), p.125.
72 Ibn al-Qayyim al Jawziyya, *Bad'iul Fawaid* 2/444.
73 Imam Abdul Wahhab Ash-Sha'rani – The Muhammadan Covenants (Unpublished).

starting from around the 3rd Islamic century. A specialised and comprehensive programme of training was undertaken by the *fāris* (trooper) who had to display,

> obedience to a superior officer; an ability to make correct military decisions; steadiness in adversity; horsemanship; nimbleness in attack; possession of good quality weapons and armour; and skill in their use... *furusiyya* exercises reflected the Muslim military elite's traditional willingness to learn from any source, some exercises having come from Khurasan in eastern Iran, others from Byzantium... They dealt with archery, use of the lance, sword and mace, wrestling, parade-ground skills, hunting, crossbow-shooting, polo and horse-riding.[74]

The scope of *Furusiyya* was extended to include specific training, exercises, and games performed on foot. *Furusiyya* was, therefore, subdivided into "upper *Furusiyya*" (*al-Furusiyya al-'ulwyah*), which denoted activities performed on horseback, and "lower *Furusiyya*" (*al-Furusiyya al-suflyah*), which denoted those performed on foot, like wielding arms, archery, boxing, and wrestling."[75]

Beyond the golden era of Prophet 🕌, his Companions and the Followers, the height of *Furusiyya* and its success lay around the time of those legends known as the "Saviours of Islamic Spirit" namely Nur al-Dīn Zangi (1118–1174) and the first sultan of Egypt and Syria and founder of the Ayyubid dynasty, Salah al-Dīn al-Ayyubi (1137–1193).[76]

The arts most notably practised alongside grappling at the time of the Messenger of God 🕌 as they relate to their practical application in warfare include:

---

74 David Nicolle, Christa Hook, *Saracen Faris*, (Reed International Books, 1994), p.9.
75 al-Sarraf, "Mamluk Furusiyah Literature and Its Antecedents," 200.
76 Abu'l Hasan Ali Nadwi, *Saviours of Islamic Spirit*, (White Thread Press, 2015).

ARCHERY

Of the martial arts practised by the Messenger of God ﷺ, archery is perhaps the most established and thoroughly documented of combat arts in the era of the early Muslims.

The Messenger of God ﷺ said: "You must use archery, for it is good for him who engages in warfare."[77]

SWORDSMANSHIP AND SPEAR FIGHTING

The Prophet ﷺ was a formidable swordsman. His blade rarely left his side, as is clear from the accounts of him delivering sermons leaning upon it and indelible records of the numerous swords he had in his ﷺ possession. Several of his personal swords have been preserved to this day[78] and as was his habit to name his possessions, they include:

i. Al-Ma'thur, which was his first sword, inherited from his father

ii. Al-Qadib

iii. Al-Qala'i

iv. Al-Battar (The Cutter)

v. Al-Hatf (Death)

vi. Al-Mikh'dham (The Slicer)

vii. Al-Rasub (The Plunging Blade)

viii. Al-Samsama (The Unbreakable Blade)

ix. Al-Lahif (The Enveloper)

x. Dhu-al-Fiqar,[79] his most famous sword

The Messenger of God ﷺ was equally skilled with the spear, as illustrated in the famous bout between him and Ubay ibn Khalaf, when the latter swore to assassinate the Prophet ﷺ and arrived at the Battle of Uḥud in full armour, intent on fulfilling his vow. It is narrated that Ubay charged at the Prophet ﷺ at

---

77 Narrated by At-Tabarani, taken from Mustafa Kani, *Sacred Archery*, translation of *Telhis-i-resailat-i-rumat*, (Himma Press, 2017).
78 Topkapi Palace Museum, *Pavilion of the Scared Relics, The Sacred Trusts*, (Tughra Books, 2009).
79 Yusuf Nabahani, *Wasa'il al-Wusul ila Shama'il al-Rasul – Muhammad: His Character and Beauty*, translated by Abdul Aziz Suraqah, (Al-Madina Institute, 2015), p.86.

the Battle of Uḥud, with the believers intercepting his path. The Prophet ﷺ ordered them to clear the way, and as Ubay galloped forward the Prophet ﷺ jumped up in a manner that left the Companions in awe and forced them to move out of the way. The Prophet ﷺ struck his spear with utmost precision into the clavicle of Ubay, leaving minimal damage and no blood. Upon falling off his horse, Ubay was surrounded by his comrades who mockingly said, "What is ailing you? It is only a scratch!" But he reminded them of what the Messenger of God ﷺ had said—"I shall kill Ubay"—crying "By Allah! If he hit me only with his spittle he would kill me! Did he not say 'I shall kill him'?" By the One in Whose Hand is my soul! If the wound I just received were in the people of Dhūl-Majāz they would all die!" He died on his way to Mecca.[80]

It was commonplace in pre- and early Islamic Arabia for tribal leaders or notable horsemen to carry more than one sword, although this was more for practical purposes than as a show of affluence.

> The sword was the early Arabs' sole close combat weapon and in the course of fighting there was a risk that it would not only get blunt but that it could be broken, especially if used against an armoured foe. For example, at the battle of Mu'ta nine swords were reportedly broken in the hand of Khalid Ibn al-Walid who was wearing several of them—though not, of course, all nine.[81]

EQUITATION

As clearly emphasised in the Qur'an in the previously mentioned verse relating to the preparation of war with "horses tethered", horsemanship was pivotal to the Messenger of God

---

80   Gibril Fouad Haddad, *Sports in Islam* (http://steppenreiter.de/sports_in_islam.htm)
81   Shihab al-Sarraf, *A Companion to Medieval Arms and Armour* (Boydell Press 2008), under Close Combat Weapons in the Early 'Abbasid Period: Maces, Axes and Swords, p.149–178. It should be noted that this section is probably one of the most authoritative works on Islamic weaponry.

⁂, his Companions and to the early Muslims. The Quranic references combined with the abundance of Prophetic statements related to horses, provide clear guidance on the beauty, virtues and import of these blessed creatures. In a recent unique and scholarly English publication,[82] the role of horses in Islam, their virtues and a comprehensive historical and modern commentary is presented:

> The Prophet Muhammad ⁂ truly loved horses and displayed his affection for them through his actions and words. Some have stated that there are approximately 2000 ahadith of his that relate to the horse.[83]

The Messenger of God ⁂ said:

> Great good is attached to the forelock of horses until the Day of Judgment, by which both reward (in the Hereafter) and booty (in this world) are gained.[84]

SWIMMING

Whilst not related to the martial arts, swimming was also heavily emphasised as a physical Prophetic practice. The Messenger of God ⁂ is said to have mastered the art of diving in the well of the clan of 'Adi ibn An-Najjār. The Messenger of God ⁂ said:

> Everything other than the remembrance of God is idle talk and heedlessness except four things: walking between two targets [during archery practice]; training his horse; entertaining his spouse; and teaching swimming.[85]

---

82 Yusuf Bemath, *Al-Asl – The Pure-bred Arabian Horse*, (Yusuf Bemath, printed by Impress Investments Ltd, 2012).
83 Ibid. p.6.
84 Ibid. p.6. Hadith found in Bukhari, 2887.
85 Al-Nasa'i, al-Bazzar, al-Tabarani, al-Baghawi, al-Diya' and others with a strong chain according to al-Haythami.

Social and Communal Recreation

He that will make good use of any part of his life must
allow a large part of it to recreation. (John Locke)

Paralleled with specific ritual acts of worship, like the con-
gregational prayer and the pilgrimage of Hajj, there was a social
objective to the sports of the Muslims. With intention providing
the basis and ultimately the reward in any given act of worship,
even the shooting of an arrow to attain mastery, the display of
a cheerful countenance to your friend or testing oneself in a
grappling contest is commendable.

Whilst one could argue that the spectacle of modern sports,
with its manipulation of statistics, manufactured drama and
addictive celebrity culture, is nefarious and creates self-delusion
in the onlookers by simplifying and devaluing the art,[86] its communal impact and social gravity is undeniable.

When honed in a setting of purpose, morality and noble endeavour, sports in general and martial arts specifically, can serve
as a positive influence in the community. Healthy competition
with the intention of self-improvement, discipline, wholesome
entertainment and adherence to virtuous conduct promotes
communal harmony.

---

86   See Chris Hedges, *Empire of Illusion – The End of Literacy and the Triumph of Spectacle*, (Nation
Books, 2009).

Upon seeing some of the Companions preoccupied in shooting arrows and having not offered their obligatory prayer, another Companion asked the Prophet ﷺ whether it would not be better for them to pray instead. To this, the Messenger of God ﷺ replied,

> Their busying themselves with the bow is as if it were part of the prayer...[87]

We also find narrations in al-Bukhāri of the Prophet ﷺ taking his family on the day of 'Id, as a means of entertainment, to watch the Abyssinians performing spear play in his presence in the *Masjid an-Nabawi*.

The Muslim world acknowledged the value of grappling as a means to instil good character, encourage the youth and provide community entertainment, occasionally hosting wrestling tournaments on festive days, weddings and religious holidays.

Early Muslim rulers introduced what became known as *"Futuwwah* clubs" in the 6th Islamic century around the Fertile Crescent. These were popularly attributed to the Abbasid caliph, al-Nāsir li-Dīn Allah, who saw communal participation in the martial arts as a means to removing inequalities in the class structure amongst Muslims as well as encouraging social responsibility. Taken from the Arabic word for "youth" (*fata*, pl. *fityān*), the *Futuwwah* clubs, as known as *akhis* (brotherhood), unwittingly served as a means of uniting Muslims of differing social stratas and were devoted to arts, "...such as crossbow shooting, wrestling, and training homing pigeons while some were mutual aid organizations. Members could include Muslims and non-Muslims. There were artisans and workers, but also the lower class or the marginalized..."[88]

---

87 Mustafa Kani, *Sacred Archery,* translation of *Telhis-i-resailat-i-rumat* (Himma Press, 2017), p.53.
88 Futuwwa:https://www.encyclopedia.com/religion/encyclopedias-almanacs-transcripts-and-maps/futuwwa

The Ottomans facilitated viable means to learn and teach wrestling in village communities across the empire,

> The Turkish word for the place in which wrestling takes places is *tekke*, which is the same word used to describe a Sufi lodge.... Each Ottoman community had its own wrestling champion. A rich man or a committee associated with the local church or mosque provided the champion with room and board in return for training the community's wrestlers... this training usually took place on property owned by a church, mosque or Sufi order...
>
> At the local level, contests took place on feast days and at weddings... A youth who did not wrestle was unlikely to be respected by his peers or marry well.[89]

Beyond the camaraderie shared between sports teammates, grappling engenders an immediate sense of brotherhood and companionship. The connection one experiences when grappling with another person is unique and deeply rooted, often cementing lifelong friendships. It is this experience that made ancient *Futuwwah* clubs or communal rites of passage successful and intimately unforgettable.

> You release the lock. You and your opponent make eye contact. You both smile and thank each other for the roll.[90] A certain understanding passes between you. You know him in a way that his co-workers and "civilian" friends never will.[91]

---

89 Thomas A. Green, *Martial Arts of the World: An Encyclopedia of History and Innovation, Vol. 2.* (ABC-CLIO, 2010). Adapted.
90 *Roll* is a term used for full sparring in a Jiu-jitsu grappling match involving submissions, locks and chokes.
91 Nicolas Gregoriades – *The Jiu-jitsu Experience.* Accessed: https://www.jiujitsubrotherhood.com/blogs/blog/a-jiu-jitsu-experience

Skilful Mastery

إِنَّ اللهَ يُحِبُّ إِذَا عَمِلَ أَحَدُكُمْ عَمَلًا أَنْ يُتْقِنَـهُ

The Messenger of God ﷺ said, "God loves a servant
who when performing a task does so skilfully."[92]

The above narration establishes the third objective of sports in
Islam. Some of the most grand and beautiful products of Islamic
civilisation spawned from this central concept of masterful conduct or *Itqān*, which should permeate every endeavour, vocation,
craft and skill. The foundation of this notion is embedded in the
Quranic description of God Himself, in the image of the mountains in creation moving imperceptibly like clouds, God says:

وَتَرَى ٱلْجِبَالَ تَحْسَبُهَا جَامِدَةً وَهِىَ تَمُرُّ مَرَّ ٱلسَّحَابِ ۚ صُنْعَ ٱللَّهِ ٱلَّذِىٓ
أَتْقَنَ كُلَّ شَىْءٍ ۚ إِنَّهُۥ خَبِيرٌۢ بِمَا تَفْعَلُونَ ۝ ٨٨:٢٧

And you see the mountains thinking they are firmly fixed, but
they will float away like clouds: this is the handiwork of God
who has perfected all things. He is fully aware of what you do.
(Qur'an, 27:88)

---

92 Hadith related by al-Bayhaqi, taken from Hamza Yusuf, *The Content of Character*, (Sandala LLC, 2005) p.24

The root of the word *Itqān* (تقن) reflects a meaning of perfection, thoroughness, exactitude, and mastery,[93] which is closely linked to the central Islamic concept of *Iḥsān*[94] (spiritual excellence).

It is *Itqān* that helped the likes of Abul Qasim Khalaf ibn-Abbas al-Zahrawi invent over 200 surgical tools used in medicine in the 10th century that are still being used today; pushed Al-Biruni to discuss the theory of the Earth rotating on its own axis 600 years before Galileo, and drove Al-Khwarizmi in the 9th century to discover Algebra. Many of Islam's architectural, geographical and technological advancements were born out of a type of precise and complete pursuit of mastery of one's craft.

> In a (Muslim) civilisation that stretched from Spain to China the golden rays of discovery and invention shone over everything. Through scholars and scientists of various faiths some of the most important discoveries known to man were made at this time.[95]

It is regrettable that in the current age of endless distraction and instant gratification that the concept and pursuit of mastery is no longer given much thought. Lamentable, given the extent some of the most luminous figures of Islamic history devoted to master not only their scholarly but also their martial pursuits.

Take, for example, the great Imam Muhammad ibn Idrīs as-Shāfʻi (150–204AH), one of the founders of the four great Sunni schools of sacred law. He is heralded as having laid the foundations of Islamic Jurisprudence,[96] a linguistic specialist and inspiring poet, yet was also a master of archery and is reported to have had such accuracy so as to write his name in shooting arrows.

---

93 J.M. Cowan, *The Hans Wehr Dictionary of Modern Written Arabic* (Spoken Language Services, 1976).
94 *Iḥsān* forms part of the classical triune of Islamic practice articulated in the famous tradition recorded in Sahih Muslim of the archangel Jibrīl (Gabriel), in which Jibril in human form visits the Prophet Muhammad ﷺ in the presence of his Companions seeking clarification on *Islam* (outward submission to God), *Imān* (Faith) and *Iḥsān* (spiritual excellence).
95 Salim T.S. Al-Hassani, *1001 Inventions – The Enduring Legacy of Muslim Civilisation*, (National Geographic Society, 2012).
96 Gibril Fouad Haddad, *The Four Imams and their Schools*, (Muslim Academic Trust, 2007), p.185.

Similarly, we recall the story of a man born blind (he recovered his sight in later life), who lost his father as an infant and was subsequently raised by his mother. He spent his entire life memorising, teaching and compiling ahadith of the Messenger of God ﷺ. He possessed a remarkable memory, allowing him to commit over three hundred thousand ahadith with their chains of transmission, and his students became the most renowned hadith scholars. He travelled the entire Muslim world in search of traditions of the Messenger of God ﷺ. In a famous incident in which he travelled to Basra, after having spent several days with the scholars of hadith, his peers rebuked him for wasting his time and not writing any notes or the narrations he had heard. Upon hearing this he asked the other students to bring their notes and he meticulously recalled each hadith he had heard from memory, and continued until he had narrated over fifteen thousand hadith. Yet, his brilliance in this field did not prevent him from attaining mastery in another; his precision in the science of hadith spilled over into the art of archery. He was a master archer, spending hours after the *Fajr* prayer refining his technique and developing laser-like accuracy. He was known never to have missed the target except twice. His name was Abū ʿAbd Allah Muhammad ibn Ismaīl al-Bukhārī.

The art of grappling provides a canvas upon which the student can witness their own progress; it also encourages, almost through necessity of survival, the development of mastery over the many and varied techniques and positions. Micro goals of overcoming training partners, learning seemingly detailed and complex techniques and drills, attaining physical strength and conditioning, and overcoming anxieties, progressively lead to more weighty objectives like competition success, fight preparation and the ability to teach. At every trough, one questions their commitment to the art. Each difficult training session and disabling injury slowly chips away at one's resolve to stay the course.

Nonetheless, it is at these individual junctures that significant progress is made. Equally, it is through the range of these collective experiences that the fortunate uncover the road of mastery.

> It resists definition yet can be instantly recognised. It comes in many varieties yet follows certain unchanging laws. It brings rich rewards, yet it is not really a goal or a destination but rather a process, a journey.[97]

Ghazi bin Muhammad mentions,

> Indeed, *Itqān* ("mastery" or right action which stems from total commitment) is considered as the fourth of the five cardinal qualities for Muslims after *Islam* (submission to God; right doctrine); *Iman* (faith; right belief) and *Iḥsān* (virtue; right worship), and before *Ikhlās* (sincerity; right being). Moreover, "mastery" is in itself the first step—and this the *sine qua non*—toward self-mastery, which is "spiritual victory" over the vices and evil of one's own ego, the reward for which is nothing other than Heaven. This also explains why, really, it is better to play well and lose than play badly and win.[98]

One of the greatest basketball players of all time, Michael Jordan, on his continued success after reaching the pinnacle of his sport remarked, "Success is enough to keep coming back." However, it is a misplaced understanding of accomplishment that increases an internal pressure to succeed, and a mistaken self-satisfaction in thinking we have attained mastery.

> With accomplishment comes a growing pressure to pretend that we know more than we do. To pretend we already know everything. *Scientia infla* (knowledge puffs up). That's the worry and the risk—thinking that we're set and secure, when in reality understanding and mastery is a fluid, continual process.[99]

---

97 George Leonard, *Mastery - The Keys to Success and Long-term Fulfilment,* (Penguin Group, 1992), p.18.
98 Ghazi bin Mohammed, *The Sacred Origins of Sports and Culture,* (Fons Vitae, 1998).
99 Ryan Holiday, *Ego is the Enemy,* (Profile Books Ltd, 2016), p.104

Remaining on this path of mastery, drawing on due parallels to any worthy endeavour, is a great challenge which claims many "lives". The symbolic death of the samurai was pronounced not when he was killed on battlefield fighting the enemy in combat, but when he stopped traversing the path, no longer training to attain mastery. When you stop your pursuit of the arts, "you are as good as dead."

Instead, sadly we find many dip their toes in the water with great enthusiasm, having researched every conceivable aspect of the art, only to give up after a few short sessions or "injuries". This is indicative of what George Leonard calls the "dabbler", which typifies most modern participants,

> When he makes his first spurt of progress in a new sport, for example, the Dabbler is overjoyed. He demonstrates his form to family, friends, and people he meets on the street. He can't wait for the next lesson. The falloff from his first peak comes as a shock. The plateau that follows is unacceptable if not incomprehensible. His enthusiasm quickly wanes. He starts missing lessons. His mind fills up with rationalizations. This really isn't the sport for him. It's too competitive, non-competitive, aggressive, non-aggressive, boring, dangerous, whatever. He tells everyone that it just doesn't fulfil his unique needs. Starting another sport gives the Dabbler a chance to replay the scenario of starting up. Maybe he'll make it to the second plateau this time, maybe not. Then it's on to something else.[100]

Duality in creation is an unspoken yet obvious reality. Our observation and acceptance of day and night, land and sea, sun and moon, sweetness and bitterness, male and female, is manifest by the immediate way we interact with them. God alludes to this,

---

100   George Leonard, *Mastery – The Keys to Success and Long-term Fulfilment*, (Penguin Group, 1992), p.20.

68

وَمِن كُلِّ شَيْءٍ خَلَقْنَا زَوْجَيْنِ لَعَلَّكُمْ تَذَكَّرُونَ ۞ ٥١:٤٩

And We created pairs of all things,
so perhaps you would be mindful. (Qur'an, 51:49)

Mastery occurs in the struggle that perpetually endures between them, the agonizing sway between opposites and how that struggle in and of itself is a proof of truth. This "struggle" of polarities was extensively studied and articulated by the ancient Greek philosopher Empedocles[101] who mentioned,

> Thus, light and darkness, darkness and light, like all the elements of nature, are destined to wrestle each other, beating and losing continuously, to a sequence where the struggle affirms the existence and the existence the struggle.[102]

This struggle exists within all realms of life. Mastery is not that path which knows not defeat or failure, but rather engenders deep pursuit despite it. Query the *Qāri* (Master reciter of the Qur'an) about his commitment to the precise and eloquent recital of the Book of God, the learning and articulation of each letter and associated vowels, the lengthening of the *maddūd*, the memorisation and application of the sacred rules of *Tajwīd* (Rules of Articulation). He will inform you that the mastery of recitation is unattainable, and despite its pursuit being immensely rewarding, is a lifelong endeavour.

We must also know that there will always be someone better, more capable than us; however, this must not deter us from the journey towards mastery. The renowned Jiu-jitsu master

101 Empedocles was an ancient Greek philosopher born in Acragas (a city in Sicily) born in 492 BC. His philosophy is eclectic, meaning that he fused multiple philosophical traditions together including the thoughts of the earlier Milesian philosophers and their understanding of the world being made up of elements. Empedocles believed the world to be made up of the four primary elements: earth, water, wind and fire. http://www.philosimply.com/philosopher/empedocles
102 Kameas, Albandis, Barbas, "The Decency of Strength and the Strength of Decency: A Philosophical Approach to the Sport of Wrestling," 11.

Chris Haueter poignantly remarked, "It's not about who is best, but rather who is left." There is a tempering between continual improvement, learning whilst erring, and knowing that eternal perfection lies with the Creator.

> Al-Bukhari narrated that when a nomad's camel outpaced the Prophet's she-camel, al-'Adhba', which was known to be always first in racing, the Muslims felt sad. The Prophet consoled them and taught them the proper demeanour in sportsmanlike support of one's team: *"Almighty God has decreed that nothing shall have a permanent glory."*[103]

Consistency and longevity are hallmarks of any worthy pursuit as "the best deeds are those done regularly even if they are few".[104] One should avoid relegating the practice of a physical art to only the young, fit or capable, inasmuch as one would not apply this mentality to their own spiritual routine. In fact, the progress gained by inculcating this as a regular practice in and of itself, would bode well for the practitioner in their spiritual strivings.

We should take heed of the above hadith and understand how our pursuit of mastery is inextricably tied to our closeness to our Creator and is ultimately linked to our commitment in the quintessential elements of our faith—like the prayer, for instance—and fulfils a core objective in the engagement of Prophetic activities.

---

103 Ghazi bin Mohammed, *The Sacred Origins of Sports and Culture*, (Fons Vitae, 1998).
104 Sunan ibn Majah, 4240.

Refreshment of Body & Soul

وَكَذَلِكَ جَعَلْنَكُمْ أُمَّةً وَسَطًا ۞ ٢:١٤٣

We have made you a justly balanced community…
(Qur'an, 2:143)

The scholars of exegesis mention that "the justly balanced (*wasat*) in reality is the furthest point between two extremes".[105] A balance between laxity and excess in all endeavours must be attained. This objective is beautifully established in no more a descriptive manner than the incident of the great companion and scribe of the Messenger of God ﷺ, Ḥanẓalah al-Usayyidī ﴾.

It is narrated in Sahih Muslim:

عَنْ حَنْظَلَةَ الأُسَيْدِيِّ - وَكَانَ مِنْ كُتَّابِ رَسُولِ اللهِ صَلَّى اللهُ عَلَيْهِ وَسَلَّمَ - قَالَ: لَقِيَنِيْ أَبُوْ بَكْرٍ فَقَالَ: كَيْفَ أَنْتَ يَا حَنْظَلَةُ؟ قَالَ قُلْتُ: نَافَقَ حَنْظَلَةُ. قَالَ: سُبْحَانَ اللهِ، مَا تَقُوْلُ؟

---

105 Imam Fakruddin al-Razi, *Al-Tafsir al-Kabir*.

قَالَ: قُلْتُ: نَكُونُ عِنْدَ رَسُولِ اللهِ صَلَّى اللهُ عَلَيْهِ وَسَلَّمَ يُذَكِّرُنَا بِالنَّارِ وَالْجَنَّةِ حَتَّى كَأَنَّا رَأْيَ عَيْنٍ، فَإِذَا خَرَجْنَا مِنْ عِنْدِ رَسُولِ اللهِ صَلَّى اللهُ عَلَيْهِ وَسَلَّمَ عَافَسْنَا الْأَزْوَاجَ وَالْأَوْلَادَ وَالضَّيْعَاتِ، فَنَسِينَا كَثِيرًا.

قَالَ أَبُو بَكْرٍ: فَوَاللهِ إِنَّا لَنَلْقَى مِثْلَ هَذَا. فَانْطَلَقْتُ أَنَا وَأَبُو بَكْرٍ حَتَّى دَخَلْنَا عَلَى رَسُولِ اللهِ صَلَّى اللهُ عَلَيْهِ وَسَلَّمَ. قُلْتُ: نَافَقَ حَنْظَلَةُ يَا رَسُولَ اللهِ.

فَقَالَ رَسُولُ اللهِ صَلَّى اللهُ عَلَيْهِ وَسَلَّمَ: وَمَا ذَاكَ؟

قُلْتُ: يَا رَسُولَ اللهِ، نَكُونُ عِنْدَكَ تُذَكِّرُنَا بِالنَّارِ وَالْجَنَّةِ حَتَّى كَأَنَّا رَأْيَ عَيْنٍ، فَإِذَا خَرَجْنَا مِنْ عِنْدِكَ عَافَسْنَا الْأَزْوَاجَ وَالْأَوْلَادَ وَالضَّيْعَاتِ، فَنَسِينَا كَثِيرًا.

فَقَالَ رَسُولُ اللهِ صَلَّى اللهُ عَلَيْهِ وَسَلَّمَ: «وَالَّذِي نَفْسِي بِيَدِهِ، إِنْ لَوْ تَدُومُونَ عَلَى مَا تَكُونُونَ عِنْدِي وَفِي الذِّكْرِ لَصَافَحَتْكُمُ الْمَلَائِكَةُ عَلَى فُرُشِكُمْ وَفِي طُرُقِكُمْ، وَلَكِنْ يَا حَنْظَلَةُ سَاعَةً سَاعَةً. ثَلَاثَ مَرَّاتٍ

Abū Bakr met and asked, "How are you Ḥanẓalah?" I replied, "Ḥanẓalah has become a hypocrite." He said, "Glory be to God! What are you saying?"

I replied, "When we are with God's Messenger 鬈, he mentions the Fire and the Garden until it is as if we can see them. But when we leave the Prophet's company and play with our wives and children or by ourselves with our properties, we forget much."

Abū Bakr 鬈 said, "By God, I have experienced the same thing." He and I then went to visit the Messenger of God 鬈 and I said, "O Messenger of God, Ḥanẓalah has become a hypocrite." He 鬈 asked, "And how is that?"

I replied, "O Messenger of God, when we are with you, you talk about the Fire and the Garden until it is as if we can see them. Then we go out and play with our wives and children and deal with our properties, and we forget much."

The Messenger of God 鬈 then said, "By Him in Whose hand is my soul, if you were to continue at the same level at which you were when with me and in remembering God, the angels would shake hands with you when you are resting and when you walk about, but O Ḥanẓalah, there is a time (for this) and a time (for that)." He repeated this phrase three times.[106]

There is much to be gained through a balance in ritual worship, acquisition of beneficial knowledge, familial responsibilities and even earning a living. Traditionally, Muslims have always considered "variety in worship" (التنوع في العبادة) occasionally changing modes and methods of supererogatory acts, to recalibrate the physical and spiritual acts of worship. Even the etymological origins of the British word "holiday" is tied to the concept of a "holy day" or "day of exemption from labour".

---

106   Sahih Muslim, 2750. Taken from Yusuf al-Qaradawi, *The Lawful and the Prohibited in Islam*, (Al-Birr Foundation, 2003), p.268.

Indeed, a proper balance of work and relaxation is the way to strengthen the soul's capacity and endurance for work, just as a proper balance of physical exercise and rest makes the body strong and fitter.[107]

The American equivalent "vacation" provides a clearer understanding of the refreshment intended here, "freedom from obligations, leisure, release", or as the Latin *vactionem* (nominative *vacatio*) indicates "leisure, freedom, exemption, a being free from duty, immunity earned by service."[108]

Roman and Greek philosophers were only too aware of the negative effects of slothfulness and embedded themselves in physical culture as a means of revitalizing and strengthening mind and body. The concept of *Mens sana in corpore sano* or "a healthy mind in healthy body" was central to the understanding of mental and psychological wellbeing.

> Everything we do here in the earthly domain has an immediate impact on the sacred and spiritual domain. A healthy body can act as nothing less than a healthy home for the numerous challenges and demands made upon the soul.[109]

In Muslim scholarly circles, the old adage "All work and no play make Jack a dull boy" is something of a lost concept. The sheer might and prodigious output of traditional Muslim scholars is impressive; even in our more idle modern times, we are treated to glimpses of the glorious past. The recent publication of a colossal forty-volume biographical dictionary on the female hadith scholars[110] of Islam by Shaykh Mohammad Akram Nadwi (God protect and preserve him), is testament to the commitment, high aspirations and lengths great minds will exert in the pursuit

107　Ghazi bin Mohammed, *The Sacred Origins of Sports and Culture*, (Fons Vitae, 1998).
108　Entries taken from https://www.etymonline.com/ - Online Etymology Dictionary.
109　Shaykh Seraj Hendricks, *Sport and Islam* - http://mysite.mweb.co.za/residents/mfj1/sport.htm
110　The title of the work *al-Muhaddithat: The Women Scholars of Islam*, (Interface Publications Ltd, 2013) is the English prefatory of a forty-volume Arabic work which was recently published in Morocco. In personal conversations with the author, Shaykh Akram Nadwi, he maintains his research still uncovers more female scholars of the past and he continues to add to his original collection.

of knowledge. However, these lofty examples are few and far between. What is witnessed increasingly is a lack of commitment and perceived value in physical activity to inform and bolster spiritual strivings.

In sum, just as the benefits of mainstream sports and physical activity for the betterment of mind and body have been acknowledged, equal consideration should be given to the physical endeavours of antiquity to strengthen and refresh us for greater service.

The blessed Companion of the Messenger of God ﷺ, Abū Darda' ؓ said,

> I entertain my heart with something trivial in order to make it stronger in the service of the truth.[111]

---

111   Ghazi bin Mohammed, *The Sacred Origins of Sports and Culture*, (Fons Vitae, 1998).

Self-Defence

عَنْ سَعِيدِ بْنِ زَيْدٍ، عَنِ النَّبِيِّ صَلَّى اللهُ عَلَيْهِ وَسَلَّمَ، قَالَ:
«مَنْ قُتِلَ دُوْنَ مَالِهِ فَهُوَ شَهِيْدٌ، مَنْ قُتِلَ دُوْنَ دِيْنَهِ
فَهُوَ شَهِيْدٌ، مَنْ قُتِلَ دُوْنَ دَمِهِ فَهُوَ شَهِيْدٌ، مَنْ قُتِلَ
دُوْنَ أَهْلِهِ فَهُوَ شَهِيْدٌ»

On the authority of Saīd ibn Zaid, the Prophet ﷺ said:

> Whoever is killed defending his property is a martyr.
> Whoever is killed defending his religion is a martyr.
> Whoever is killed defending his life is a martyr. Whoever
> is killed defending his family is a martyr.[112]

With the exception of intellect, all of the major objectives
(*maqāsid*) that are to be preserved by the sacred law of Islam
(*Shari'ah*) are contained within the above narration, namely religion, self, children and wealth.[113]

It is without doubt that the men and women around the
Messenger of God ﷺ belonged to a warrior nation; they were
people well-acquainted with confrontation and warfare. Tribal

---

112   Sunan al-Tirmidhi, 1421.
113   Mohammad Hashim Kamali, *Principles of Islamic Jurisprudence*, (The Islamic Texts Society, 2003).

feuds, drawn out conflicts between neighbouring Bedouins, and lifelong vendettas were commonplace prior to the advent of Islam, naturally spilling over into the time of the Prophet ﷺ and his Companions. Historic accounts are rich with details of aggressive disputes and the exchange of blood money upon the death of a slain man.

Whilst arguments could be made with regards to the most effective means of self-preservation or defence, the above narration not only establishes a definitive objective for the study of grappling but also provides a compelling incentive to those contemplating embarking on a journey through the Prophetic martial arts, or questions the very purpose of it.

The value and effectiveness of a given martial art is unfortunately not proportionate to the currency it enjoys among the masses, and thus a highly effective art form may not prove to be particularly popular. This is certainly the case for wrestling specifically and grappling more generally; however, this is slowly changing with the indispensability of the grappling arts like wrestling, sambo and Jiu-jitsu in modern Mixed Martial Arts. Likewise, unfamiliarity tends to place a restriction on uptake and popularity, and this is precisely the case with the Muslim Ummah in its leaving or forgetting the great heritage of the past, particularly with regards to certain well-established Prophetic practices.

قَالَ رَسُولُ اللهِ صَلَّى اللهُ عَلَيْهِ وَسَلَّمَ: «إِنَّمَا الأَعْمَالُ بِالنِّيَّةِ. وَإِنَّمَا لِكُلِّ امْرِئٍ مَا نَوَى. فَمَنْ كَانَتْ هِجْرَتُهُ إِلَى اللهِ وَرَسُولِهِ فَهِجْرَتُهُ إِلَى اللهِ وَرَسُولِهِ. وَمَنْ كَانَتْ هِجْرَتُهُ لِدُنْـيَا يُـصِـيْـبُـهَا أَوِ امْـرَأَةٍ يَـتَـزَوَّجُـهَا فَهِجْرَتُهُ إِلَى مَا هَاجَرَ إِلَيْهِ

As has been established by the Messenger of God ﷺ in a well-known hadith:

> Verily, deeds are only by intentions. Verily, every person will have only what they intended. Whoever emigrated to God and His Messenger, then his emigration is for God and His Messenger. Whoever emigrated to get something in the world or to marry a woman, then his emigration is for whatever he emigrated for.[114]

It is through this statement that God's acceptance and appropriated reward to the believer of a given action is established.

The one engaged in a definitive Prophetic practice (*Sunnah*) is ultimately engaged in an act of worship for the duration of that time and is likewise rewarded for it. It would greatly restrict the broad meaning of the above hadith to limit its application to only ritual worship (prayer, charity, etc.). Scholars of hadith commenting upon this narration clarify the fact that the establishment of intention is critical to our existence, for it can render all actions praiseworthy and rewardable or abhorrent and sinful. The mercy instituted through this has the potential to render a seemingly minor action great by a noble intention, or conversely, cause a grand action to be abased by a corrupt intention.

There are numerous examples of this nature explicitly given by the Messenger of God ﷺ. In the context of martial combat specifically, a clear example is found in the noble art of archery.

On the authority of Abū Darda' ؓ the Prophet ﷺ said,

> Everyone who walks between the two points of the archery field, will have merited the reward for a good deed for every step he takes.[115]

As such, despite any definitive evidence of the precise form of grappling the Prophet ﷺ engaged in and encouraged, grappling

---

114 Bukhari & Muslim.
115 Narrated by At-Tabarani. Taken from Mustafa Kani, *Sacred Archery*, translation of *Telhis-i-resailat-i-rumat*, (Himma Press, 2017), p.37.

could likewise be considered a form of worship with the correct intention. Arguably, if the primary objective of wrestling at that time was to prepare one for military engagement or self-defence, then a case could be made for the practising of other styles of grappling that equally constitute a fulfilment of the Prophetic practice.

It is this practice, the Prophetic practice—which some will ridicule, scoff at, question and others believe to be redundant—that remains. It remains for reasons we may or may not appreciate, yet is cherished in the limbs, hearts, and souls of courageous people, who truly acknowledge that paragon ﷺ sent by the Divine, as the one whose every word, deed and action is pregnant with meaning and deep wisdom.

Perhaps through walking the physical path of the Prophet ﷺ, we uncover a spiritual means to gain closeness to the One whom he calls us to and that we grapple with that wisdom wherever we may find it as we deservedly should, to seek His pleasure, proximity, and reward. An even stronger argument could be made to practise other, more applicable martial arts within the grappling genre, which would further enhance practicality in a combative situation.

PART IV

Al-Musār'ah ilā al-Muṣār'ah
Swiftly to Wrestling

Imam Jalāl Ad-Dīn As-Suyūṭī ﷺ
(849AH–911AH)

Al-Musārʿah ilā al-Muṣārʿah, written by the great Imam Jalāl Ad-Dīn as-Suyūṭī ☙, appears to be the only classical treatise on the wrestling of the Messenger of God ☙ and his noble Companions, according to the author's knowledge. Imam as-Suyūṭī is renowned for his prodigious scholarly output—he was said to have written three volumes a day—conceivably writing on every major and subsidiary branch of Islamic thought. Alongside his major titles, as-Suyūṭī's minor short booklets, of which *Al-Musārʿah* is one, have often served to highlight the nuances of the deeply cultured, often peculiar nature of Muslim life. The eighteen narrations presented here by as-Suyūṭī, whilst being present within the major Sunni hadith compilations, are of varying degrees of textual authenticity and chains of transmission back to the Messenger of God ☙ according to the Scholars of Hadith (*Muhaddithūn*). This is characteristic of the writings of as-Suyūṭī, for which Islamic scholars have on occasion criticised him for. Due to the slight divergence of the *Muhaddithūn* upon the narrations presented, it is beyond the scope of the present work to categorise the narrations further.

The annotations and comments provided below each narration are solely by the author of this book, through the consultation of acknowledged and traditionally trained Muslim scholars.

NARRATION 1

الحديث الأول

عَنْ أَبِيْ جَعْفَرِ بْنِ مُحَمَّدِ بْنِ عَلِيِّ بْنِ رُكَانَةَ عَنْ أَبِيْهِ أَنَّ رُكَانَةَ
صَارَعَ النَّبِيَّ صَلَّى اللهُ عَلَيْهِ وَسَلَّمَ، فَصَرَعَهُ النَّبِيُّ.

(أخرجه أبو داود والترمذي، كذا في المسارعة للسيوطي)

On the authority of Abī Jaʿfar ibn Muhammad ibn
ʿAli ibn Rukānah ☙ narrates that, his father Rukānah
wrestled the Messenger of God ☙ and he ☙ took him
down. (*Abū Dawūd and Tirmidhī*)

الحديث الثاني

عَنْ مُحَمَّدِ بْنِ رُكَانَةَ عَنْ أَبِيْهِ أَنَّ رُكَانَةَ صَارَعَ النَّبِيَّ صَلَّى اللهُ
عَلَيْهِ وَسَلَّمَ، فَصَرَعَهُ النَّبِيُّ.

(أخرجه أبو الحسين بن قانع في «معجمه»، كذا في المسارعة
للسيوطي)

On the authority of Muhammad ibn Rukānah ﷺ narrates
that, his father Rukānah wrestled the Messenger of God
ﷺ and he ﷺ took him down. (*ibn Qaani – al Mu'jam*)

Narrations 1 and 2 firmly establish the Prophetic practice of
grappling. Details of this encounter can be found in the following
narrations.

NARRATION 3

الحديث الثالث

عَنِ ابْنِ إِسْحَاقَ - صَاحِبِ الْـمَغَازِيْ وَالسِّيَرِ - قال: حَدَّثَنِيْ
إِسْحَاقُ بْنُ يَسَارٍ أَنَّ رَسُوْلَ اللهِ صَلَّى اللهُ عَلَيْهِ وَسَلَّمَ قَالَ
لِرُكَانَةَ بْنِ عَبْدِ يَزِيْدَ: «أَسْلِمْ». فَقَالَ: «لَوْ أَعْلَمُ أَنَّ مَا تَقُوْلُ
حَقٌّ لَفَعَلْتُهُ»، فَقَالَ لَهُ رَسُوْلُ اللهِ صَلَّى اللهُ عَلَيْهِ وَسَلَّمَ - وَكَانَ
رُكَانَةُ مِنْ أَشَدِّ النَّاسِ: «أَرَأَيْتَ إِنْ صَرَعْتُكَ، أَتَعْلَمُ أَنَّ ذَلِكَ
حَقٌّ؟»، فَقَالَ «نَعَمْ»، فَقَامَ رَسُوْلُ اللهِ صَلَّى اللهُ عَلَيْهِ وَسَلَّمَ
فَصَرَعَهُ، فَقَالَ لَهُ «عُدْ يَا مُحَمَّدُ»، فَعَادَ لَهُ رَسُوْلُ اللهِ صَلَّى اللهُ
عَلَيْهِ وَسَلَّمَ، فَأَخَذَهُ الثَّانِيَةَ، فَصَرَعَهُ عَلَى الأَرْضِ، فَانْطَلَقَ
رُكَانَةُ وَهُوَ يَقُوْلُ: «هَذَا سَاحِرٌ لَمْ أَرَ مِثْلَ سِحْرِ هَذَا قَطُّ، وَاللهِ
مَا مَلَكْتُ مِنْ نَفْسِيْ شَيْئًا حِيْـنَ وَضَعْتُ جَنْبِيْ إِلَى الأَرْضِ»

(أخرجه البيهقي في «دلائل النبوة»، كذا في المسارعة)

On the authority ibn Isḥāq —the scholar of Prophetic biography and battles—related that, The Messenger of God said to Rukānah 'Abd Yazīd, "Accept Islam." He replied, "Had I considered what you say to be true, I would have done it (i.e. accepted Islam)." The Messenger of God then said to Rukānah, the strongest one of the strongest people, "If I were to take you down, would you consider Islam to be true?" He replied, "Yes." The Messenger of God then stood up (to wrestle him) and took him down. He said to him,

"Again O Muhammad." The Messenger of God ﷺ thus stood once more and for a second time, wrestled him down to the ground. Rukānah then left saying, "This is a sorcerer. I have never seen such sorcery. I swear by God, I had absolutely no control over myself when you took me to the ground." (*al-Bayhaqi – Dalail al-Nubuwwah*)

Muhammad ibn Isḥāq ibn Yasār ibn Khiyār ﷺ, the renowned historian and founder of the discipline of *Sīra* (biographical study of the Prophet's ﷺ life), brings a fuller narration to the Prophet's ﷺ encounter with Rukānah ibn Abī Yazīd.

Rukānah ibn 'Abd Yazid ibn Hāshim ibn Muttalib ibn 'Abd Manāf-al-Qurayshi was a Companion of the Messenger of God ﷺ who accepted Islam in the year of the Conquest of Mecca in 8AH and died in Medīnah during the caliphate of Muāwīyiah in 42AH (according to *Isābah* of ibn Hajar, *Isti'aab* of ibn 'Abdi'l Barr, *Taratib al-Idariyyah* of Abd-al Hayy al-Kattani and *Silat al-Riyādati* of Sayyid Muḥammad ibn 'Alawi).

This duel is initiated upon the scepticism of faith. It is probable that this "discussion" of accepting Islam between them may have occurred on a previous occasion. The multiple and deeply inspiring narrations of how the Companions ﷺ accepted Islam at the blessed hands of the Messenger of God ﷺ are varied and nuanced. What is witnessed in this particular narration is a testimony to the Prophet's ﷺ wise manner of "speaking to people in their own tongues". Rukānah is a man of combat and physicality, seemingly only receptive to the "physical language" for which the Messenger of God ﷺ promptly obliges.

الحديث الرابع

عَنْ رُكَانَةَ بْنِ عَبْدِ يَزِيدَ - وَكَانَ رُكَانَةُ مِنْ أَشَدِّ النَّاسِ، قَالَ: «كُنْتُ أَنَا وَالنَّبِيُّ صَلَّى اللهُ عَلَيْهِ وَسَلَّمَ فِي غُنَيْمَةٍ لِأَبِي طَالِبٍ نَرْعَاهَا فِي أَوَّلِ مَا رَأَى إِذْ قَالَ لِي ذَاتَ يَوْمٍ: «هَلْ لَكَ أَنْ تُصَارِعَنِي؟»، قُلْتُ لَهُ: «أَنْتَ؟!؟»، قَالَ: «أَنَا!»، فَقُلْتُ: «عَلَى مَاذَا؟»، قَالَ: «عَلَى شَاةٍ مِنَ الْغَنَمِ»، فَصَارَعْتُهُ فَصَرَعَنِي، فَأَخَذَ مِنِّي شَاةً، ثُمَّ قَالَ لِي: «هَلْ لَكَ فِي الثَّانِيَةِ»، قُلْتُ: «نَعَمْ»، فَصَارَعْتُهُ، فَصَرَعَنِي وَأَخَذَ مِنِّي شَاةً، فَجَعَلْتُ أَلْتَفِتُ هَلْ يَرَانِي إِنْسَانٌ، فَقَالَ: «مَا لَكَ؟» قُلْتُ: «لَا يَرَانِي بَعْضُ الرُّعَاةِ فَيَجْتَرِئُونَ عَلَيَّ وَأَنَا فِي قَوْمِي مِنْ أَشَدِّهِمْ»، فَقَالَ: «هَلْ لَكَ فِي الصِّرَاعِ الثَّالِثَةِ وَلَكَ شَاةٌ؟» قُلْتُ: «نَعَمْ»، فَصَارَعْتُهُ فَصَرَعَنِي، فَأَخَذَ شَاةً.

فَقَعَدْتُ كَئِيبًا حَزِينًا، فَقَالَ: «مَا لَكَ؟» قُلْتُ: «إِنِّي أَرْجِعُ إِلَى عَبْدِ يَزِيدَ وَقَدْ أَعْطَيْتُ ثَلَاثًا مِنْ غَنَمِهِ؛ وَالثَّانِيَةُ أَنِّي كُنْتُ أَظُنُّ أَنِّي أَشَدُّ قُرَيْشٍ، فَقَالَ: «هَلْ لَكَ فِي الرَّابِعَةِ؟»، فَقُلْتُ «لَا بَعْدَ ثَلَاثٍ»، فَقَالَ: أَمَّا قَوْلُكَ فِي الْغَنَمِ فَإِنِّي أَرُدُّهَا عَلَيْكَ، فَرَدَّهَا عَلَيَّ، فَلَمْ يَلْبَثْ أَنْ ظَهَرَ أَمْرُهُ، فَأَتَيْتُهُ فَأَسْلَمْتُ، فَكَانَ مِمَّا هَدَانِيَ اللهُ أَنِّي عَلِمْتُ أَنَّهُ لَمْ يَصْرَعْنِي يَوْمَئِذٍ بِقُوَّتِهِ، وَلَمْ

يَصْرَعَنِيْ يَوْمَئِذٍ إِلَّا بِقُوَّةٍ غَيْرِهِ.

(أخرجه البيهقي في «الدلائل»، كذا في المسارعة للسيوطي)

On the authority of Rukānah ibn 'Abd Yazīd (God be pleased with him), one of the strongest people. He relates, The Prophet ﷺ and I would graze a flock of sheep belonging to Abū Ṭālib in the initial days when he saw me. He ﷺ said to me one day, "Would you like to wrestle me?" I retorted, "You?!" He ﷺ replied, "Yes, me!" I asked him, "For what?" He ﷺ replied, "For a sheep from the flock." So, I wrestled him ﷺ and he ﷺ took me down. He ﷺ then took a sheep from me. Then he ﷺ asked me, "Would you like another round?" I replied, "Yes." So I wrestled him ﷺ and he ﷺ took me down. He ﷺ then took a sheep from me. I began looking around anxiously to see if anyone saw me. He ﷺ asked, "What's the matter with you?" I replied, "No shepherd should see me. For if they do, they will become emboldened against me, [even though they know] I am one of the strongest in my clan." He ﷺ asked, "Would you like a third round and a sheep?" I replied, "Yes." So I wrestled him, he ﷺ took me down and thereafter took a sheep. I sat down broken and in despair.

He ﷺ thus asked, "What's the matter?" I replied, "I will be returning to 'Abd Yazīd having given away three of his sheep. Secondly, I certainly thought I was the strongest of Quraysh." He ﷺ asked, "Would you like a fourth round?" I replied, "No, (not after) three rounds." So he ﷺ said, "As for what you have said regarding the sheep, I will return them to you." Thereupon, he ﷺ returned them to me. When his matter (i.e. Prophecy) manifested not much later, I came to him ﷺ and accepted Islam. From the guidance God gave me is that I knew he ﷺ did not throw me down that day by his ﷺ own strength, but rather he ﷺ only threw me down on that day with someone else's strength. (*al-Bayhaqi – Dala'il al-Nubuwwah*)

The renowned traditionist (*Muhaddith*), Abd-al Hayy al-Kattani in his work *Taratib al-Idariyyah* commenting on this narration mentions that this apparent "wager" is to be understood as from the elect allowances (*khasāis*) of the Messenger of God ﷺ and not to be misconstrued as gambling or betting. Of the seven-variant transmissions of this narration—found in various hadith collections such as Tirmidhī, Abū Dawūd, Bayhaqi, Abū Nu'aym and others—some indicate the wager being from one sheep, ten sheep and none. This hadith is narrated by Rukānah ibn Abī Yazīd ﷺ himself once again.

What is noteworthy about this narration from a grappler's perspective, is the successive nature in which the Messenger of God ﷺ is able to outwrestle and take down such a physically gifted and reputable wrestler. In the realm of high-level grappling, such repetitive success is indicative of complete mastery of the art.

Scouring countless hours of modern footage of live sparring and competitive bouts amongst some of the most accomplished grapplers in world, reveals a single unabated truth: the ability to successfully apply the same technique upon a resisting and capable individual—even amongst the most hotly contested and long-standing rivalries—is near impossible.

Methodical strategies, technical trickery and even outright foul play will be employed to achieve victory in modern-day grappling events but witnessing graceful and recurrent victories of one proponent over another is rare. It is inconceivable for a competent grappler, let alone a master wrestler, to be outdone by the same opponent more than once, without offering strong resistance.

The narration illustrates the excellence of the Messenger of God ﷺ as a supreme grappler, whilst also displaying his ﷺ magnanimity towards his defeated opponent through the reimbursement of the wager, a mere excuse to engage with such a man who went on to embrace the faith of Islam.

الحديث الخامس

عَنْ أَبِي أُمَامَةَ قَالَ: «كَانَ رَجُلٌ مِنْ بَنِيْ هَاشِمٍ، يُقَالُ لَهُ رُكَانَةُ -
وَكَانَ مِنْ أَشَدِّ النَّاسِ وأَفْتَكِهِمْ وَكَانَ مُشْرِكًا - وَكَانَ يَرْعَى غَنَمًا
لَهُ فِي وَادٍ يُقَالُ لَهُ: "إضَمُّ"، فَخَرَجَ نَبِيُّ اللهِ صَلَّى اللهُ عَلَيْهِ
وَسَلَّمَ ذَاتَ يَوْمٍ وَتَوَجَّهَ قِبَلَ ذَلِكَ الْوَادِيْ، فَلَقِيَهُ رُكَانَةُ - وَلَيْسَ
مَعَ النَّبِيِّ صَلَّى اللهُ عَلَيْهِ وَسَلَّمَ أَحَدٌ - فَقَامَ إِلَيْهِ رُكَانَةُ، فَقَالَ:
«يَا مُحَمَّدُ، أَنْتَ الَّذِي تَشْتِمُ آلِهَتَنَا اللَّاتَ وَالْعُزَّى وَتَدْعُو إِلَى
إِلَهِكَ الْعَزِيزِ الْحَكِيمِ، وَلَوْلَا رَحِمٌ بَيْنِي وَبَيْنَكَ مَا كَلَّمْتُكَ
الْكَلَامَ حَتَّى أَقْتُلَكَ، وَلَكِنِ ادْعُ إِلَهَكَ الْعَزِيزَ الْحَكِيمَ يُنْجِيكَ
مِنِّي الْيَوْمَ، وَسَأَعْرِضُ عَلَيْكَ أَمْرًا. هَلْ لَكَ أَنْ أُصَارِعَكَ وَتَدْعُو
إِلَهَكَ الْعَزِيزَ الْحَكِيمَ يُعِينُكَ عَلَيَّ وَأَنَا أَدْعُوْ اللَّاتَ وَالْعُزَّى، فَإِنْ
أَنْتَ صَرَعْتَنِي فَلَكَ عَشْرٌ مِنْ غَنَمِي هَذِهِ تَخْتَارُهَا؟»

فَقَالَ عِنْدَ ذَلِكَ النَّبِيُّ صَلَّى اللهُ عَلَيْهِ وَسَلَّمَ: «نَعَمْ، إِنْ شِئْتَ».
فَاتَّخَذَا وَدَعَا النَّبِيُّ صَلَّى اللهُ عَلَيْهِ وَسَلَّمَ إِلَهَهُ الْعَزِيزَ الْحَكِيمَ
أَنْ يُعِينَهُ عَلَى رُكَانَةَ، وَدَعَا رُكَانَةُ اللَّاتَ وَالْعُزَّى: «أَعِنِّي الْيَوْمَ
عَلَى مُحَمَّدٍ»، فَأَخَذَهُ النَّبِيُّ صَلَّى اللهُ عَلَيْهِ وَسَلَّمَ فَصَرَعَهُ
وَجَلَسَ عَلَى صَدْرِهِ.

فَقَالَ رُكَانَةُ: «قُمْ، فَلَسْتَ أَنْتَ الَّذِي فَعَلْتَ بِي هَذَا، إِنَّمَا فَعَلَهُ إِلَهُكَ الْعَزِيزُ الْحَكِيمُ - وَخَذَلَهُ اللَّاتُ وَالْعُزَّى - وَمَا وَضَعَ أَحَدٌ قَطُّ جَنْبِي قَبْلَكَ»، فَقَالَ رُكَانَةُ: «عُدْ، فَإِنْ أَنْتَ صَرَعْتَنِي فَلَكَ عَشْرُ أُخْرَى تَخْتَارُهَا»، فَأَخَذَهُ النَّبِيُّ صَلَّى اللهُ عَلَيْهِ وَسَلَّمَ وَدَعَا كُلُّ وَاحِدٍ مِنْهُمَا إِلَهَهُ كَمَا فَعَلَا أَوَّلَ مَرَّةٍ، فَصَرَعَهُ النَّبِيُّ صَلَّى اللهُ عَلَيْهِ وَسَلَّمَ وَجَلَسَ عَلَى كَبِدِهِ.

فَقَالَ لَهُ رُكَانَةُ: «قُمْ، فَلَسْتَ أَنْتَ الَّذِي فَعَلْتَ بِي هَذَا، إِنَّمَا فَعَلَهُ إِلَهُكَ الْعَزِيزُ الْحَكِيمُ - وَخَذَلَهُ اللَّاتُ وَالْعُزَّى - وَمَا وَضَعَ أَحَدٌ قَطُّ جَنْبِي قَبْلَكَ». ثُمَّ قَالَ رُكَانَةُ: «عُدْ، فَإِنْ أَنْتَ صَرَعْتَنِي فَلَكَ عَشْرٌ أُخْرَى تَخْتَارُهَا»، فَأَخَذَهُ النَّبِيُّ صَلَّى اللهُ عَلَيْهِ وَسَلَّمَ الثَّالِثَةَ، فَقَالَ لَهُ رُكَانَةُ: «لَسْتَ أَنْتَ الَّذِي فَعَلْتَ بِي هَذَا، إِنَّمَا فَعَلَهُ إِلَهُكَ الْعَزِيزُ الْحَكِيمُ - وَخَذَلَهُ اللَّاتُ وَالْعُزَّى - فَدُونَكَ ثَلَاثِينَ شَاةً مِنْ غَنَمِي، فَاخْتَرْهَا». فَقَالَ النَّبِيُّ صَلَّى اللهُ عَلَيْهِ وَسَلَّمَ: «مَا أُرِيدُ ذَلِكَ، وَلَكِنْ أَدْعُوكَ إِلَى الْإِسْلَامِ».

وَقَالَ أَبُو بَكْرٍ وَعُمَرُ: «يَا رَسُولَ اللهِ، أَصَرَعْتَ رُكَانَةَ؟! فَلَا وَالَّذِي بَعَثَكَ بِالْحَقِّ مَا نَعْلَمُ أَنَّهُ وَضَعَ جَنْبَهُ إِنْسَانٌ قَطُّ»، فَقَالَ النَّبِيُّ صَلَّى اللهُ عَلَيْهِ وَسَلَّمَ: «إِنِّي دَعَوْتُ رَبِّي؛ أَعَانَنِي بِبُضْعَ عَشَرَةٍ وَقُوَّةِ عَشَرَةٍ».

On the authority of Abū Umāma ﷺ said that, there was a man from Banū Hāshim named Rukānah. He was one of the strongest and deadliest men, and a polytheist. He used to graze his sheep in a valley called Idam. The Messenger of God ﷺ went out one day and headed toward Idam, where he ﷺ was met by Rukānah alone. So Rukānah came towards him ﷺ and said, "O Muhammad! Are you the one that insults our gods al-Lāt and al-'Uzzā, and call unto your Almighty and All-Wise God? If it wasn't for the blood relationship between you and me, I would have killed you without even uttering a word to you. However, I invite you to call unto 'your God' that is Almighty and All-Wise to save you from me today. Let me make a proposal:

What do you think about me wrestling you, with you calling unto your All-mighty and All-wise God to help you against me and my calling unto al-Lāt and al-'Uzzā? If you overcome me then I will give you, from these sheep of mine, ten of your choice."

Thereupon, the Messenger of God ﷺ said, "Yes, if you wish." They began wrestling, each trying to hold the other and throw him down, and the Messenger of God ﷺ called unto his Almighty and All-Wise God to help him against Rukānah, who called unto al-Lāt and al-'Uzzā, "Help me today against Muhammad." The Prophet ﷺ then grabbed him, took him down and sat on his chest.

Rukānah said, "Stand up, as it was not you that did this to me. Rather your Almighty and All-Wise God did this;"—and al-Lāt and al-'Uzzā had forsaken him—"no one before you has ever thrown me down." Rukānah continued, "Wrestle me again and if you take me down then I will give you another ten of your choice." So the

Prophet ﷺ took him on and each called upon their God as they had done the first time. The Prophet ﷺ then threw him down and sat on his abdomen.

Rukānah said to him ﷺ, "Stand up, as it was not you that did this to me. Rather your Almighty and All-Wise God did this;"—and al-Lāt and al-'Uzzā had forsaken him—"no one before you has ever thrown me down." Then Rukānah said, "Come again! If you throw me down, you can take another ten of your choice. After the Prophet ﷺ took him on a third time, Rukānah said to him, "You did not do this to me. This was only done by your Almighty and All-Wise God;"—and al-Lāt and al-'Uzzā had forsaken him—"Take thirty sheep from my flock: choose them." The Prophet ﷺ said, "I don't want that, rather I call you to Islam."

(Upon hearing of the encounter) Abū Bakr ﷺ and 'Umar ﷺ said, "O Messenger of God! You threw down Rukānah?! We swear by He who sent you with the truth we do not know of anyone who ever threw him down." The Prophet ﷺ said, "I sought help from my Lord. He has aided me with the potency and strength of ten (men)." (al-Bayhaqi & Abū Nu'aym - Dala'il al-Nubuwwah)

This narration is a truncated version of a longer narration brought forward by Abū Nu'aym in *Maarifat as-Sahabah* and al-Bayhaqi in *Dalail al-Nubuwwah*. However, the longer version—found at the end of this note in full—has several textual weaknesses associated with it according to hadith scholars, which again is beyond the scope of this work. There are differences of opinion with regards to when and where the wrestling bout took place, and when Rukānah accepted Islam.

The differing narrations (*riwayāh*) mention that the bout between the Messenger of God ﷺ and Rukānah took place in the following locations:

i. Bathaa near Mecca (narrated by Saīd ibn Jubayr found in Abū Dawūd)
ii. "Grazing grounds of Abū Tālib" near Mecca (al-Bayhaqi)
iii. Idam near Medīnah (Abū Nuʿaym)
iv. Mecca (narrated by Ibn ʿAbbās found in Al-Balādhuri)

It is conceivable that the Messenger of God ﷺ wrestled Rukānah ؓ on more than one occasion at different locations. In sum, in addition to the above variants, contemporary scholars (such as al-Kattani) overwhelmingly assert that the bout took place in Mecca.

Similarly, all of the narrations that pertain to Rukānah wrestling with the Messenger of God ﷺ indicate the bout occurred whilst the former had yet to accept Islam. The majority opinion is that Rukānah became Muslim at the conquest of Mecca (8AH), indicating that they wrestled in the early days of Islam before migration.

Like many hadith of the Messenger of God ﷺ, it firstly reminds us of the deep concern of the Prophet ﷺ to guide humanity. God informs us that:

$$ لَقَدْ جَآءَكُمْ رَسُولٌ مِّنْ أَنفُسِكُمْ عَزِيزٌ عَلَيْهِ مَا عَنِتُّمْ حَرِيصٌ عَلَيْكُم بِالْمُؤْمِنِينَ رَءُوفٌ رَّحِيمٌ ١٢٨:٩ $$

A Messenger has come to you from among yourselves. Your suffering distresses him: he is deeply concerned for you and full of kindness and mercy towards the believers.
(Qur'an, 9:128)

The Messenger of God ﷺ is driven by an unrelenting concern to deliver his noble message and guide people to goodness, even in the face of death.

Physical confrontation is at the peak of man's pyramid of fear. The unsettling and terrifying feeling that is associated with confronting another man is, for some, unbearable. The psychological elements of fear, particularly in the realm of combat, have been commented upon and investigated by sports psychologists and behavioural physiologists for centuries. In the world of professional boxing and mixed martial arts, even non-professional combat sports athletes enlist the aid of qualified psychologists to prepare them for the "big fight". The mental and physical stress and anxiety associated with the pending doom of a confrontation can leave people physically drained, depressed, overwhelmed and completely incapacitated.[116] The reality of physical violence, even for the seasoned martial artist, is unnerving and takes tremendous courage to overcome.

This hadith also highlights not only the martial competence of the Messenger of God ﷺ, but more so the unflinching valour and fearlessness with which he confronts this seemingly disastrous situation.

The narration further confirms the miraculous physical strength and conditioning of the Messenger of God ﷺ.

> The Prophet ﷺ wrestled others besides Rukānah, such as Abū al-Aswad al Jumahi, who was so strong that he could stand on a cow hide and ten men would try to pull the hide from under his feet, but it would be torn to bits without him moving one inch. The Prophet ﷺ challenged him to a wrestling match and Abū al-Aswad said, "If you defeat me, I will believe in you." But when the Messenger of God wrestled him and defeated him he did not confess faith.[117]

116   For an insightful understanding of real fight psychology refer to – Geoff Thomson, *The Art of Fighting without Fighting*, (Summerdale Publishers Ltd, 1998)
117   Yūsuf Nabahāni, *Wasā 'il al-Wusūl ilā Shamā ''il al-Rasūl – Muhammad His Character and Beauty*, translated by Abdul Aziz Suraqah (Al-Medīnah Institute, 2015) p.55

Narration of Abū Nuʿaym in full:

عَنْ أَبِي أُمَامَةَ، قَالَ: «كَانَ رَجُلٌ يُقَالُ لَهُ رُكَانَةُ، وَكَانَ مِنْ أَفْتَكِ النَّاسِ وَأَشَدِّهِمْ، وَكَانَ مُشْرِكًا، وَكَانَ يَرْعَى غَنَمًا لَهُ فِي وَادٍ يُقَالُ لَهُ أَضَمُ.

فَخَرَجَ نَبِيُّ اللهِ صَلَّى اللهُ عَلَيْهِ وَسَلَّمَ مِنْ بَيْتِ عَائِشَةَ ذَاتَ يَوْمٍ، فَتَوَجَّهَ قِبَلَ ذَلِكَ الْوَادِي، فَلَقِيَهُ رُكَانَةُ وَلَيْسَ مَعَ نَبِيِّ اللهِ أَحَدٌ، فَقَامَ إِلَيْهِ رُكَانَةُ فَقَالَ: «يَا مُحَمَّدُ. أَنْتَ الَّذِي تَشْتِمُ آلِهَتَنَا اللَّاتَ وَالْعُزَّى، وَتَدْعُوْ إِلَى إِلَهِكَ الْعَزِيزِ الْحَكِيمِ. لَوْلَا رَحِمٌ بَيْنِي وَبَيْنَكَ مَا كَلَّمْتُ الْكَلَامَ، يَعْنِي: حَتَّى أَقْتُلَكَ. وَلَكِنِ ادْعُ إِلَهَكَ الْعَزِيزَ الْحَكِيمَ يُنْجِيكَ مِنِّي الْيَوْمَ.

وَسَأَعْرِضُ عَلَيْكَ أَمْرًا، هَلْ لَكَ إِنْ صَارَعْتُكَ وَتَدْعُوْ إِلَهَكَ الْعَزِيزَ الْحَكِيمَ فَيُعِينُكَ عَلَيَّ وَأَنَا أَدْعُو اللَّاتَ وَالْعُزَّى؟ فَإِنْ صَرَعْتَنِي فَلَكَ عَشْرٌ مِنْ غَنَمِيْ هَذِهِ تَخْتَارُهَا».

فَقَالَ عِنْدَ ذَلِكَ نَبِيُّ اللهِ صَلَّى اللهُ عَلَيْهِ وَسَلَّمَ: «نَعَمْ، إِنْ شِئْتَ»، فَاتَّحَدَا.

فَدَعَا نَبِيُّ اللهِ إِلَهَهُ الْعَزِيزَ الْحَكِيمَ أَنْ يُعِينَهُ عَلَى رُكَانَةَ، وَدَعَا رُكَانَةُ اللَّاتَ وَالْعُزَّى: «أَعِنِّي الْيَوْمَ عَلَى مُحَمَّدٍ».

فَأَخَذَهُ النَّبِيُّ صَلَّى اللهُ عَلَيْهِ وَسَلَّمَ، فَصَرَعَهُ وَجَلَسَ عَلَى صَدْرِهِ. فَقَالَ رُكَانَةُ: «قُمْ، فَلَسْتَ الَّذِي فَعَلْتَ بِي هَذَا، إِنَّمَا إِلَهُكَ الْعَزِيزُ الْحَكِيمُ، وَخَذَلَنِي اللَّاتُ وَالْعُزَّى.وَمَا وَضَعَ جَنْبِي أَحَدٌ قَبْلَكَ.»

فَقَالَ لَهُ رُكَانَةُ: «فَإِنْ صَرَعْتَنِي فَلَكَ عَشْرٌ مِنْ غَنَمِي هَذِهِ تَخْتَارُهَا.»

فَأَخَذَهُ نَبِيُّ اللهِ صَلَّى اللهُ عَلَيْهِ وَسَلَّمَ،وَدَعَا كُلَّ وَاحِدٍ مِنْهُمَا إِلَهَهُ كَمَا فَعَلَا أَوَّلَ مَرَّةٍ، فَصَرَعَهُ النَّبِيُّ صَلَّى اللهُ عَلَيْهِ وَسَلَّمَ وَجَلَسَ عَلَى كَبِدِهِ.

فَقَالَ لَهُ رُكَانَةُ: «لَسْتَ الَّذِي فَعَلْتَ بِي هَذَا، إِنَّمَا فَعَلَهُ إِلَهُكَ الْعَزِيزُ الْحَكِيمُ، وَخَذَلَنِي اللَّاتُ وَالْعُزَّى.وَمَا وَضَعَ جَنْبِي أَحَدٌ قَبْلَكَ.»

فَقَالَ رُكَانَةُ: «فَإِنْ صَرَعْتَنِي فَلَكَ عَشْرٌ أُخْرَى تَخْتَارُهَا.»

فَأَخَذَهُ نَبِيُّ اللهِ صَلَّى اللهُ عَلَيْهِ وَسَلَّمَ، وَدَعَا كُلَّ وَاحِدٍ مِنْهُمَا إِلَهَهُ كَمَا فَعَلَا أَوَّلَ مَرَّةٍ، فَصَرَعَهُ النَّبِيُّ صَلَّى اللهُ عَلَيْهِ وَسَلَّمَ الثَّالِثَةَ.

فَقَالَ لَهُ رُكَانَةُ: «لَسْتَ الَّذِي فَعَلْتَ بِي هَذَا، إِنَّمَا فَعَلَهُ إِلَهُكَ الْعَزِيزُ الْحَكِيمُ، وَخَذَلَنِي اللَّاتُ وَالْعُزَّى.»

فَدُونَكَ ثَلَاثِينَ شَاةً مِنْ غَنَمِي فَاخْتَرْهَا. فَقَالَ لَهُ النَّبِيُّ صَلَّى اللهُ عَلَيْهِ وَسَلَّمَ: «مَا أُرِيدُ ذَلِكَ، وَلَكِنْ أَدْعُوكَ إِلَى الْإِسْلَامِ يَا رُكَانَةُ. وَأَنْفَسُ بِكَ أَنْ تَصِيرَ إِلَى النَّارِ، إِنَّكَ إِنْ تُسْلِمْ تَسْلَمْ.»

فَقَالَ لَهُ رُكَانَةُ: «لَا، إِلَّا أَنْ تُرِيَنِي آيَةً»

فَقَالَ لَهُ نَبِيُّ اللهِ صَلَّى اللهُ عَلَيْهِ وَسَلَّمَ: «اللهُ عَلَيْكَ شَهِيدٌ، لَئِنْ أَنْ دَعَوْتُ رَبِّي فَأَرَيْتُكَ آيَةً لَتُجِيبُنِي إِلَى مَا أَدْعُوكَ إِلَيْهِ؟» قَالَ: «نَعَمْ» وَقَرِيبٌ مِنْهُمَا شَجَرَةُ سَمُرٍ ذَاتُ فُرُوعٍ وَقُضْبَانٍ. فَأَشَارَ إِلَيْهَا نَبِيُّ اللهِ صَلَّى اللهُ عَلَيْهِ وَسَلَّمَ وَقَالَ لَهَا: «أَقْبِلِي بِإِذْنِ اللهِ.»

فَانْشَقَّتْ بِاثْنَيْنِ، فَأَقْبَلَتْ عَلَى نِصْفِ سَاقِهَا وَقُضْبَانِهَا وَفُرُوعِهَا حَتَّى كَانَتْ بَيْنَ يَدَيْ نَبِيِّ اللهِ وَبَيْنَ رُكَانَةَ. فَقَالَ لَهُ رُكَانَةُ: «أَرَيْتَنِي عَظِيمًا، فَمُرْهَا فَلْتَرْجِعْ».

فَقَالَ لَهُ نَبِيُّ اللهِ صَلَّى اللهُ عَلَيْهِ وَسَلَّمَ: «اللهُ عَلَيْكَ شَهِيدٌ، إِنْ أَنَا دَعَوْتُ رَبِّي، ثُمَّ أَمَرْتُهَا فَرَجَعَتْ لَتُجِيبُنِي إِلَى مَا

أَدْعُوكَ إِلَيْهِ؟» قَالَ: «نَعَمْ»

فَأَمَرَهَا، فَرَجَعَتْ بِقُضْبَانِهَا وَفُرُوعِهَا حَتَّى إِذَا الْتَأَمَتْ بِشِقِّهَا، فَقَالَ لَهُ النَّبِيُّ صَلَّى اللهُ عَلَيْهِ وَسَلَّمَ: «أَسْلِمْ تَسْلَمْ».

فَقَالَ لَهُ رُكَانَةُ: «مَا بِي إِلَّا أَنْ أَكُونَ قَدْ رَأَيْتُ عَظِيمًا، وَلَكِنِّي أَكْرَهُ أَنْ تَسَامَعَ نِسَاءُ الْمَدِينَةِ وَصِبْيَانُهُمْ أَنِّي إِنَّمَا أَجَبْتُكَ لِرُعْبٍ دَخَلَ قَلْبِي مِنْكَ، وَلَكِنْ قَدْ عَلِمَتْ نِسَاءُ الْمَدِينَةِ وَصِبْيَانُهُمْ أَنَّهُ لَمْ يُوضَعْ جَنْبِي قَطُّ وَلَمْ يَدْخُلْ قَلْبِي رُعْبٌ سَاعَةً قَطُّ لَيْلًا وَلَا نَهَارًا، وَلَكِنْ دُونَكَ، فَاخْتَرْ غَنَمَكَ.»

فَقَالَ لَهُ النَّبِيُّ صَلَّى اللهُ عَلَيْهِ وَسَلَّمَ: «لَيْسَ بِي حَاجَةٌ إِلَى غَنَمِكَ إِذَا أَبَيْتَ أَنْ تُسْلِمَ.» فَانْطَلَقَ نَبِيُّ اللهِ صَلَّى اللهُ عَلَيْهِ وَسَلَّمَ رَاجِعًا وَأَقْبَلَ أَبُو بَكْرٍ وَعُمَرُ رَضِيَ اللهُ تَعَالَى عَنْهُمَا يَلْتَمِسَانِهِ فِي بَيْتِ عَائِشَةَ، فَأَخْبَرَتْهُمَا أَنَّهُ قَدْ تَوَجَّهَ قِبَلَ وَادِي أَضَمَ، وَقَدْ عَرَفَا أَنَّهُ وَادِي رُكَانَةَ لَا يَكَادُ يُخْطِئُهُ.

فَخَرَجَا فِي طَلَبِهِ وَأَشْفَقَا أَنْ يَلْقَاهُ رُكَانَةُ فَيَقْتُلُهُ. فَجَعَلَا يَتَصَاعَدَانِ عَلَى كُلِّ شَرَفٍ وَيَتَشَرَّفَانِ لَهُ إِذْ نَظَرَا نَبِيَّ اللهِ صَلَّى اللهُ عَلَيْهِ وَسَلَّمَ مُقْبِلًا. فَقَالَا: «يَا نَبِيَّ اللهِ. كَيْفَ تَخْرُجُ إِلَى هَذَا الْوَادِي وَحْدَكَ وَقَدْ عَرَفْتَ أَنَّهُ جِهَةُ رُكَانَةَ، وَأَنَّهُ مِنْ

١٠٠

أَقْتَلِ النَّاسِ وَأَشَدِّهِمْ تَكْذِيبًا لَكَ؟» فَضَحِكَ إِلَيْهِمَا، ثُمَّ قَالَ: «أَلَيْسَ يَقُولُ اللهُ تَعَالَى لِي: ((وَاللهُ يَعْصِمُكَ مِنَ النَّاسِ))؟ [المائدة: ٦٧]

إِنَّهُ لَمْ يَكُنْ يَصِلُ إِلَيَّ وَاللهُ مَعِي».

فَأَنْشَأَ يُحَدِّثُهُمَا حَدِيثَ رُكَانَةَ، وَالَّذِي فَعَلَهُ بِهِ وَالَّذِي أَرَاهُ، فَعَجَبًا مِنْ ذَلِكَ، فَقَالَا: «يَا رَسُولَ اللهِ، أَصَرَعْتَ رُكَانَةَ؟ فَلَا وَالَّذِي بَعَثَكَ بِالْحَقِّ، مَا وَضَعَ جَنْبَيْهِ إِنْسَانٌ قَطُّ».

فَقَالَ النَّبِيُّ صَلَّى اللهُ عَلَيْهِ وَسَلَّمَ: «إِنِّي دَعَوْتُ اللهَ رَبِّي، فَأَعَانَنِي عَلَيْهِ. وَإِنَّ رَبِّي أَعَانَنِي بِبِضْعَ عَشَرَةَ وَبِقُوَّةِ عَشَرَةٍ».

On the authority of Abū Umāma who said that there was a man from Banū Hāshim named Rukānah. He was one of the strongest and deadliest men, and a polytheist. He used to graze his sheep in a valley called Idam.

The Messenger of God ﷺ went out one day from the house of Āʾisha and headed toward Idam, where he ﷺ was met by Rukānah alone.

So Rukānah came towards him ﷺ and said, "O Muhammad! Are you the one that insults our deities al-Lāt and al-ʿUzzā, and calls towards your Almighty and All-Wise God? If it wasn't for the blood relationship between you and me, I would have killed you without even uttering a word to you. However, I invite you to call unto 'your God' that is Almighty and All-Wise to save you from me today. Let me make a proposal: What do you think about me wrestling you, with you calling unto your All-mighty and All-wise God to help you against me and my calling unto al-Lāt and al-ʿUzzā? If you overcome me then I will give you, from these sheep of mine, ten of your choice." Thereupon, the Messenger of God ﷺ said, "Yes, if you wish."

They began wrestling, each trying to hold the other and throw him down, and the Messenger of God ﷺ called unto his Almighty and All-Wise God to help him against Rukānah, who called unto al-Lāt and al-ʿUzzā, "Help me today against Muhammad."

The Prophet ﷺ then grabbed him, took him down and sat on his chest.

Rukānah said, "Stand up, as it was not you that did this to me. Rather your Almighty and All-Wise God did this—and al-Lāt and al-ʿUzzā have forsaken me—no one before you has ever thrown me down." Rukānah continued, "Wrestle me again and if you take me down then I will give you another ten of your choice."

So the Prophet ﷺ took him on and each called upon their deities as they had done the first time. The Prophet ﷺ then threw him down and sat on his abdomen.

Rukānah said to him ﷺ, "Stand up, as it was not you that did this to me. Rather your Almighty and All-Wise God did this—and al-Lāt and al-ʿUzzā have forsaken me—no one before you has ever thrown me down." Then Rukānah said, "Come again! If you throw me down, you can take another ten of your choice. After the Prophet ﷺ took him down for a third time Rukānah said to him, "You did not do this to me. This was only done by your Almighty and All-Wise God—and al-Lāt and al-ʿUzzā have forsaken me. Take thirty sheep from my flock: choose them."

The Prophet ﷺ said, "I don't want that, rather I call you to Islam and I am reluctant to allow you to go to the Hell-fire. If you submit (to Islam), you will be saved" So, Rukānah said to him, "No, unless you show me a sign."

The Prophet ﷺ then said to him, "God is a witness. If I was to call unto my Lord and show you a sign, would you respond to that which I call you to?" Rukānah responded, "Yes."

Near them was a brown tree with branches and leaves. So, the Prophet pointed to the tree and said, "Come, with the permission of God."

So, it broke itself into two and walked on its roots, branches and leaves until it was in front of the Prophet ﷺ and Rukānah.

Then, Rukānah said to the Prophet ﷺ, "You've shown me something amazing. Tell it to return."

The Prophet ﷺ then said to him, "God is a witness. If I was to call unto my Lord and show you a sign, would you respond to that which I call you to?"

He responded, "Yes." So, he ﷺ commanded it and it returned in its entirety to its original position— rejoining its two halves together. The Prophet ﷺ said, "Submit (to Islam) and you will be saved."

Then Rukānah said to him, "Indeed, I have surely seen something great; however, I dislike the idea that the children and women of Medīnah will gossip about me that I accepted your call due to fear of you that entered my heart. However, the women and children of Medīnah know that I've never been taken down and fear has never entered my heart. So, here you go! Choose your sheep."

So, then the Prophet ﷺ said, "I have no need for your sheep if you refuse to accept Islam."

So, the Prophet ﷺ left whilst Abū Bakr and 'Umar arrived, searching for him in the house of Ā'isha. She told them that the Prophet ﷺ had gone to the valley of Idam. They knew it was the valley of Rukānah and that the Prophet ﷺ would have to pass through it. So, they went out looking for him ﷺ. They hoped to meet Rukānah in order to kill him. They traversed high peaks in their journey.

Suddenly, they saw the Prophet ﷺ coming towards them so they both said, "Why did you go to this valley alone? Whilst you know it is the valley of Rukānah and he is the deadliest of men and an ardent opponent of yours?"

So, the Prophet ﷺ laughed at them and then said, "Didn't God say to me that 'God shall protect you from the people?'[118] He won't be able to do anything to me as long as God is with me."

Then the Prophet ﷺ narrated the story of what transpired between him and Rukānah, and the miracles that ensued. This amazed Abū Bakr and 'Umar. (Upon hearing of the encounter) Abū Bakr and 'Umar said, "O Messenger of God! You threw down Rukānah!? We swear by He who sent you with the truth we do not know of anyone who ever threw him down."

The Prophet ﷺ said, "I sought help from my Lord. He has aided me with the potency and strength of ten."

---

118 Qur'an, 5:67.

الحديث السادس

عَنْ عَبْدِ اللهِ بْنِ مَسْعُودٍ أَنَّ رَجُلًا لَقِيَ شَيْطَانًا فِي سِكَّةٍ مِنْ سِكَكِ الْمَدِينَةِ، فَصَارَعَهُ فَصَرَعَهُ، فَقَالَ: «دَعْنِيْ وَأُخْبِرُكَ بِشَيْءٍ يُعْجِبُكَ، فَوَدَعَهُ». فَقَالَ: «هَلْ تَقْرَأُ سُوْرَةَ الْبَقَرَةِ؟»، قَالَ: «نَعَمْ»، قَالَ: «فَإِنَّ الشَّيْطَانَ لَا يَسْمَعُ مِنْهَا شَيْءٌ إِلَّا أَدْبَرَ وَلَهُ خَبَجٌ كَخَبَجِ الْحِمَارِ»، فَقِيْلَ لِابْنِ مَسْعُودٍ: «مَنْ ذَاكَ الرَّجُلُ؟»، قَالَ: «عُمَرُ بْنُ الْخَطَّابِ».

(أخرجه أبو عُبيد في «فضائل القرآن»، والدارمي في «مسنده»، والطبراني في «المعجم الكبير»، وأبو نعيم والبيهقي كلاهما في «دلائل النبوة»، كذا في المسارعة)

On the authority of 'Abd Allāh ibn Mas'ūd ﷺ said that,
A man met a devil in one of the alley ways of Medīnah,
whom he wrestled and defeated. The devil said, "Leave
me and I will tell you something you will like." So the
man left him. The devil then said, "Do you recite Sūrah
al-Baqarah?" The man replied, "Yes". The devil [then]
said, "If the devil hears any of it, he runs away breaking
wind like that of a donkey." It was then asked of Ibn
Mas'ūd, "Who was that man?" He replied, "Umar ibn al-
Khattāb ﷺ." (*Abū Ubayd - Fadāil al Qur'an, al Darami,
- Musnad al-Darami, al-Tabarani Mu'jam al Kabīr, al-
Bayhaqi & Abū Nu'aym - Dala'il al-Nubuwwah*)

This narration highlights the plotting and cowardice of Satan who persistently "lies in wait for the offspring of Adam along his paths."[119] The promise of Satan is mentioned in the Qur'an: "I will come at them—from their front and their back, from their right and their left."[120]

The appearance of Satan in physical form, as many other narrations describe, is indicative of the various guises and ruses he adopts, depending on the faith of the victim at hand. In other words, there appears to be a gradient in the attacks deployed by Satan, ranging from insidious whisperings (*waswasa*) to adopting various physical forms. The Companions also witnessed such transmutations of Satan: Abū Hurayrah ﷺ seeing Satan in the form of a man (Bukhāri, see note 6); Mu'ādh ibn Jabal ﷺ, an elephant (Tabarani); Ubayy ibn Ka'b ﷺ, a young boy (Ibn Hibbān); and Abū Sa'īd al-Khudrī ﷺ, a snake (Muslim).

We are also informed of an instance at the Battle of Badr in which Satan approached the Quraysh in the form of a man, Surāqah ibn Mālik ﷺ, who assured them of help as they were to fight the Muslims. As the battle approached, Satan fled—an event which is alluded to in the Qur'an:

> Satan made their foul deeds seem fair to them, and said, "No one will conquer you today, for I will be right beside you," but when the armies came within sight of one another he turned on his heels, saying, "This is where I leave you: I see what you do not, and I fear God—God is severe in His punishment."[121]

Scholars indicate that the breaking of wind by Satan relates to his desire to mask the sound of the recitation of Qur'an or due to the fear felt by Satan at the time. Other similar incidents are recorded, for instance, the Messenger of God ﷺ says:

---

119   In the wording of the hadith in Sunan al-Nasā'i 3134 - إِنَّ الشَّيْطَانَ قَعَدَ لِابْنِ آدَمَ بِأَطْرُقِهِ
120   Qur'an, 7:17.
121   Qur'an, 8:48.

"When the call to prayer (*adhān*) is pronounced, Satan takes to his heels and passes wind with noise (ضــرط) during his flight so as not to hear the call to prayer."[122]

'Umar ibn al-Khaṭṭāb ﷺ, the second Caliph of Islam, a senior companion of the Messenger of God ﷺ about whom the Prophet ﷺ mentioned:

يَا ابْنَ الْخَطَّابِ، وَالَّذِي نَفْسِي بِيَدِهِ مَا لَقِيَكَ الشَّيْطَانُ سَالِكًا
فَجًّا إِلاَّ سَلَكَ فَجًّا غَيْرَ فَجِّكَ

O son of Khaṭṭāb, by the one in whose hand is my soul, whenever Satan sees you taking a path, then he will take another path.[123]

'Umar was tall, strong and athletic. He was a robust and vigorous man who was ambidextrous. The great historian Al-Baladhuri[124] accounts he practised Genealogy, Wrestling, Oration and Horsemanship. 'Umar was a formidable wrestler that fought in the wrestling field of 'Ukāz.[125]

Satan, as mentioned in this narration, is a reality from which believers seek refuge, as attested to by God: "Indeed, Satan is an enemy to you; so, take him as an enemy."[126]

---

122 Sahih Bukhari, 608.
123 Sahih Bukhari, 6085.
124 Ahmad ibn Yahya al- Balādhuri was a 9th century Muslim historian. One of the eminent Middle Eastern historians of his age, he spent most of his life in Baghdad and enjoyed great influence at the court of the caliph al-Mutawakkil. He travelled in Syria and Iraq, compiling information for his major works.
125 Al-Balādhuri, *Kitāb al-Ashrāf*, as highlighted in Shibli Numani, Al-Farooq, *The life of Omar the Great*, translated by Maulana Zafar Ali Khan, (Adam Publishers & Distributors, 2003).
126 Qur'an, 35:6.

NARRATION 7

الحديث السابع

عَنْ عَمَّارِ بْنِ يَاسِرٍ، قَالَ: «أَرْسَلَنِيَ النَّبِيُّ صَلَّى اللهُ عَلَيْهِ وَسَلَّمَ
إِلَى بِئْرٍ، فَلَقِيتُ الشَّيْطَانَ فِي صُورَةِ الإِنْسِ، فَقَاتَلَنِي، فَصَرَعْتُهُ،
ثُمَّ جَعَلْتُ أَدُقُّهُ بِفِهْرٍ مَعِيْ أَوْ حَجَرٍ، فَقَالَ النَّبِيُّ صَلَّى اللهُ
عَلَيْهِ وَسَلَّمَ: «لَقِيَ عَمَّارٌ الشَّيْطَانَ عِنْدَ الْبِئْرِ، فَقَاتَلَهُ» فَمَا عَدَا
أَنْ رَجَعْتُ، فَأَخْبَرْتُهُ، قَالَ: «ذَاكَ الشَّيْطَانُ».

(أخرجه أبو نعيم والبيهقي وصححه، كذا عند السيوطي في
المسارعة)

On the authority of 'Ammār ibn Yāsir ﷺ said that, the
Messenger of God ﷺ sent me to a well and I met the devil
in the form of a human. He fought me and I wrestled
him down. I then began pounding him with a large
stone that I had with me. Meanwhile, the Messenger of
God ﷺ said (informing of his companions), "Ammār
met the devil at the well and fought him." As soon as I
returned, I informed him ﷺ. He ﷺ said, "That was the
devil." (*Abū Nuʿaym & al-Bayhaqi*)

Scholars indicate that the description of meeting the devil in
a human form could be indicative of:

i. Thwarting of the devil.
ii. A humiliation of the devil by God through creation.

iii. The devil being present near those desirous elements of worldly life (i.e. in this case the water well).

iv. Creation's continuous battle against him.

The devil taking on a human form is commonly observed in many traditions; a notable hadith found in al-Bukhāri mentions a similar case;

> Abū Hurayrah ﷺ reported: The Messenger of God ﷺ put me in charge of the charity of Ramadān (*Sadaqat-ul-Fitr*).
>
> Somebody came to me and began to take away some food-stuff. I caught him and said, "I must take you to the Messenger of God ﷺ." He said, "I am a needy man with a large family, and so I have a pressing need." I let him go.
>
> When I saw the Messenger of God ﷺ the next morning, he asked me, "O Abū Hurayah! What did your captive do last night?" I said, "O Messenger of God! He complained of a pressing need and a big family. I felt pity for him so I let him go." He ﷺ said, "He told you a lie and he will return."
>
> I was sure, according to the saying of the Messenger of God ﷺ that he would return. I waited for him. He sneaked up again and began to steal food-stuff from the charity. I caught him and said; "I must take you to the Messenger of God ﷺ." He said, "Let go of me, I am a needy man. I have to bear the expenses of a big family. I will not come back." So I took pity on him and let him go.
>
> I went at dawn to the Messenger of God ﷺ who asked me, "O Abū Hurayrah! What did your captive do last night?" I replied, "O Messenger of God! He complained of a pressing want and the burden of a big family. I took pity on him and so I let him go." He ﷺ said, "He told you a lie and he will return."
>
> (That man) came again to steal the food-stuff. I apprehended him and said, "I must take you to the Messenger of God ﷺ, and this is the last of three times.

You promised that you would not come again but you did." He said, "Let go of me, I shall teach you some words with which God may benefit you." I asked, "What are those words?" He replied, "When you go to bed, recite the Verse of the Throne (Ayat-ul-Kursi, 2:255) for there will be a guardian appointed over you from God, and Satan will not be able to approach you till morning." So I let him go.

Next morning the Messenger of God ﷺ asked me, "What did your prisoner do last night?" I answered, "He promised to teach me some words which he claimed will benefit me before God. So I let him go."

The Messenger of God ﷺ asked, "What are those words that he taught you?" I said, "He told me: 'When you go to bed, recite *[none has the right to be worshipped but He, the Ever Living, the One Who sustains and protects all that exists. Neither slumber nor sleep overtakes Him. To Him belongs whatever is in the heavens and whatever is on the earth. Who is he that can intercede with Him except with His Permission? He knows what happens to them (His creatures) in this world, and what will happen to them in the Hereafter. And they will never encompass anything of His Knowledge except that which He wills. His Throne encompasses the heavens and the earth and preserving them does not fatigue Him. And He is the Most High, the Most Great].*'[127]

He added: 'By reciting it, there will be a guardian appointed over you from God who will protect you during the night, and Satan will not be able to come near you until morning.'"

The Messenger of God ﷺ said, "Verily, he has told you the truth though he is a liar. O Abū Hurayrah! Do you know with whom you were speaking for the last three nights?" I said, "No." He ﷺ said, "He was the devil."[128]

---

127   Qur'an, 2:255.
128   Riyād as-Sālihīn – Hadith 1020.

الحديث الثامن

عَنْ عَمَّارِ بْنِ يَاسِرٍ، قَالَ: «قَاتَلْتُ مَعَ رَسُوْلِ اللهِ صَلَّى اللهُ
عَلَيْهِ وَسَلَّمَ الإِنْسَ وَالْجِنَّ»، قُلْنَا: «كَيْفَ قَاتَلْتَ الْجِنَّ؟»، قَالَ:
«نَزَلْنَا مَعَ رَسُوْلِ اللهِ صَلَّى اللهُ عَلَيْهِ وَسَلَّمَ مَنْزِلًا، فَأَخَذْتُ
قِرْبَتِيْ وَدَلْوِيْ لِأَسْتَقِيَ، فَقَالَ لِيْ رَسُوْلُ اللهِ صَلَّى اللهُ عَلَيْهِ
وَسَلَّمَ: «أَمَا أَنَّهُ سَيَأْتِيْكَ آتٍ يَمْنَعُكَ عَنِ الْـمَـاءِ»، فَلَمَّا كُنْتُ
عَلَى رَأْسِ الْبِئْرِ إِذَا رَجُلٌ أَسْوَدُ كَأَنَّهُ مِرْسٌ. فَقَالَ: «لَا وَاللهِ لَا
تَسْتَقِيْ الْيَوْمَ مِنْهَا ذَنُوْبًا وَاحِدًا، فَأَخَذْتُهُ وَأَخَذَنِيْ، فَصَرَعْتُهُ
ثُمَّ أَخَذْتُ حَجَرًا فَكَسَرْتُ بِهِ أَنْفَهُ وَوَجْهَهُ، ثُمَّ مَلَأْتُ قِرْبَتِيْ،
فَأَتَيْتُ بِهَا رَسُوْلَ اللهِ صَلَّى اللهُ عَلَيْهِ وَسَلَّمَ، فَقَالَ: «هَلْ أَتَاكَ
عَلَى الْـمَـاءِ مِنْ أَحَدٍ؟ فَأَخْبَرْتُهُ»، قَالَ: «ذَاكَ الشَّيْطَانُ».

(أخرجه ابن سعد في «الطبقات» وإسحاق بن راهويه في
«مسنده»، كذا في المسارعة)

On the authority of 'Ammār ibn Yāsir ﷺ said that, I
fought in the company of the Messenger of God ﷺ both
human and Jinn. We were asked, "How did you fight
the Jinn?" I replied, "We set camp at a place with the
Messenger of God ﷺ and then I took my waterskin and
bucket to fetch water." The Messenger of God ﷺ said
to me, "Someone will come to you to block you from
the water." So, when I was at the foot of the well, I saw

a black man who seemed quite strong. This man said to me, "No, by God, you will not fetch a single bucketful of water today." So, I grabbed him, and he grabbed me, and I took him down. Then I took a rock and, with it, shattered his nose and face. Thereafter, I filled my waterskin and brought it to the Messenger of God ﷺ. He ﷺ asked, "Did anyone come to you at the water?" I told him what had occurred. He ﷺ then said, "That was the devil." (*Ibn Sa'd, Musnad –Ishaq ibn Rāhawayh*)

For the Western reader in the modern context, the terms "black" man (and "slave" in Narration 9) are loaded terms that carry negative connotations. However, the mention of a black man and his connection to Satan in this narration is not to be misconstrued as having any racial connotations.

> Arabness and blackness were not viewed as mutually exclusive in early Islamic history. By blackness in this context is not an identity which has been framed as inferior compared to whiteness in the colonial and post-colonial periods but relating to physical traits such as brown or black which can also include curly or kinky hair texture. In fact, the predominant description of Arabs was within the framework of non-white complexion. This point is illustrated in a number of classical Islamic texts both explicitly and implicitly.[129]

Any and all types of prejudice and bigotry in faith are levelled when God reminds us, "The most noble of you in the sight of God are those God-conscious of you." (Qur'an, 49:13). Likewise, the Prophet ﷺ informs us that, "Verily God does not look at your appearance or wealth, rather He looks at your hearts and actions."[130] In his memorable final sermon, the Prophet ﷺ definitively declares:

129 Ahmad Mubarak & Dawud Walid – *Centering Black Narrative – Black Muslim Nobles Among the Early Pious Muslims Vol.1* (Itrah Press 2016, 2018).
130 Sahih Muslim, 2564.

There is no superiority of an Arab over a non-Arab or non-Arab over an Arab, or white (person) over a black (person) or black (person) over white (person), except by piety.[131]

The Prophet ﷺ worked tirelessly to rid the pre-Islamic racial and tribal prejudices present at his time. This is evidenced through even a cursory look at his ﷺ noble life and family.

i.   Ali ibn Abī Tālib—the Prophet's paternal cousin—is said by majority description to have been black in skin colour (ādam shahīd al-udma).[132]

ii. His adopted son Zayd ibn Hāritha ﷺ— about whom the Prophet ﷺ remarked "Bear witness that Zayd is my son!"—was a black man. He was also a military commander who was entrusted with leading the Muslim armies in many expeditions including the Battle of Mutah where his force of 3,000 faced the Byzantine Army of 200,000.

iii. Baraka bint Tha'laba ﷺ, also known as Umm Ayman, a woman who was deeply loved by and who cared for the Prophet ﷺ in his youth, and about whom he ﷺ affectionately referred to as "My mother after my mother", was a black woman of Ethiopian African descent.

iv. Bilāl ibn Rabāh al-Habashī ﷺ, the famous black Ethiopian companion, who was much-loved by the Prophet ﷺ and by whom he was appointed the principal role as mu'adhin (Prayer Caller) and treasurer, one the most esteemed public roles in Islam.

African men[133] at the time of the Prophet ﷺ were renowned for their physical strength, bravery and wrestling abilities; this

---

131   Musnad Ahmad, 23489.
132   Ahmad Mubarak & Dawud Walid – *Centering Black Narrative – Black Muslim Nobles Among the Early Pious Muslims -vol.1 & Ahl al-Bayt, Blackness & Africa - vol.2* (Itrah Press 2016, 2018)
133   Incidentally, as-Suyūtī has a separate work (Kitāb Raf' Sha'n al-Hubshān - *Risen Status of the Abyssinians*) dedicated to the virtues of the African Peoples. Refer to Saud H. al-Kathlan, A Critical Edition of Kitāb Raf' Sha'n al-Hubshān by Jalāl al-Din-al-Suyūtī (University of St Andrews, 1983 – http://hdl.handle.net/10023/2921). This work is based on an early work by Ibn Jawzī, *Kitāb Tanwīr al-Ghabash* (Illuminating the Darkness: On the Merits of Blacks and Ethiopians). A recent

is also evidenced by the specific noun in the narration *mirsun* (مرس) indicative of "one being trained" or a warrior. The specific mention of a "black man" in this narration is thus no more than a description and a highlighting of an immensely strong adversary in terms of physical prowess.

The narrator of the hadith is none other than the great 'Ammar ibn Yāsir ﷺ, known as one of the seven earliest Muslims to announce their faith in public who were subjected to immense torture by the Quraysh. It was said that the following verse was revealed by God due to the suffering of 'Ammar, "Whoever disbelieves in God after having believed in Him, except one who is coerced, whilst his heart rests securely in faith."[134]

'Ammar migrated to Medīnah and was present at the Battles of Badr, Uḥud and Khandaq and was the first person to build a mosque in Islam; namely Masjid al-Quba in Medīnah. He was appointed as governor of Kūfah by 'Umar ibn al-Khaṭṭāb ﷺ and was killed during the caliphate of 'Ali ibn Abī Tālib ﷺ in the Battle of Siffīn at the age of ninety-four. 'Ammar is described as being tall in stature, black in skin colour and having kinky hair.[135]

translation has become publicly available, see *The Spirits of Black Folk: Sages Through the Ages* (Celebrate Mercy, 2021). Also see Imran Hamza Alawiye, Ibn Jawzi's *Apologia On Behalf of the Black People and Their Status in Islam* – A Critical Edition and Translation of Kitāb Tanwīr al-Ghabash fī Faḍl al-Sūdan wa-l-Habash (School of Oriental And African Studies, 1985). For an insightful and linguistic understanding refer to Zaid Shakir, '*Islam, The Prophet Muhammad, and Blackness*', Seasons (Journal of Zaytuna Institute – Spring–Summer Reflections 2005). Similarly, recent publications by Ahmad Mubarak and Dawud Walid *Centering Black Narrative – Black Muslim Nobles Among the Early Pious Muslims* Vols. 1 & 2 (Itrah Press 2016, 2018) along with *Blackness and Islam* (Islamic Human Rights Commission 2021) by Dawud Walid, categorically affirm 'Blackness' as a historical reality within the family and descendants of the Prophet Muhammad ﷺ.
134   Qur'an, 16:106.
135   Al-Hakim, al-Mustadrak ala as-Sahihayn, 5650.

الحديث التاسع

عَنْ عَلِيِّ بْنِ أَبِي طَالِبٍ، قَالَ: «كُنَّا مَعَ النَّبِيِّ صَلَّى اللهُ عَلَيْهِ
وَسَلَّمَ فِي سَفَرٍ، فَقَالَ - صَلَّى اللهُ عَلَيْهِ وَسَلَّمَ - لِعَمَّارٍ: «انْطَلِقْ
فَاسْتَقِ لَنَا مِنَ الْمَاءِ»، فَانْطَلَقَ فَعَرَضَ لَهُ شَيْطَانٌ فِي صُورَةِ
عَبْدٍ أَسْوَدَ، فَحَالَ بَيْنَهُ وَبَيْنَ الْمَاءِ، فَصَرَعَهُ عَمَّارٌ، فَقَالَ لَهُ:
«دَعْنِي وَأُخْلِ بَيْنَكَ وَبَيْنَ الْمَاءِ» فَفَعَلَ، ثُمَّ أَتَى فَأَخَذَهُ عَمَّارٌ
الثَّانِيَةَ فَصَرَعَهُ، فَقَالَ: «دَعْنِي وَأُخْلِ بَيْنَكَ وَبَيْنَ الْمَاءِ»
فَفَعَلَ، ثُمَّ أَتَى فَأَخَذَهُ عَمَّارٌ الثَّالِثَةَ فَصَرَعَهُ، فَقَالَ رَسُولُ اللهِ
صَلَّى اللهُ عَلَيْهِ وَسَلَّمَ: «إِنَّ الشَّيْطَانَ قَدْ حَالَ بَيْنَ عَمَّارٍ
وَبَيْنَ الْمَاءِ فِي صُورَةِ عَبْدٍ أَسْوَدَ، وَإِنَّ اللهَ أَظْفَرَ عَمَّارًا بِهِ،
قَالَ عَلِيٌّ: «فَتَلَقَّيْنَا عَمَّارًا فَأَخْبَرْنَاهُ بِقَوْلِ رَسُولِ اللهِ صَلَّى اللهُ
عَلَيْهِ وَسَلَّمَ، فَقَالَ: «أَمَا وَاللهِ لَوْ شَعَرْتُ أَنَّهُ شَيْطَانٌ لَقَتَلْتُهُ».

(أخرجه أبو الشيخ ابن حيان في كتاب «العظمة»، وأبو نعيم
في «الدلائل» و«معرفة الصحابة»، كذا في المسارعة للسيوطي)

On the authority of ʿAli ibn Abī Ṭālib ﷺ said that, We
were with the Messenger of God ﷺ on a journey when
he said to ʿAmmār ﷺ, "Go and fetch us some water." He
went but (as he drew near) a devil in the form of a black
slave obstructed him and tried to bar him from the
water. So ʿAmmār ﷺ wrestled him down. The devil then

said to him, "Let me go and I will not obstruct you from the water." He relented but soon after he came again, so ʿAmmār ⚜ wrestled him down. He then said, "Let me go and I will not obstruct you from the water." Again he relented. But a few moments later he came again, so ʿAmmār ⚜ grabbed him a third time and took him down. (As this was happening), the Messenger of God ﷺ said, "The devil came between ʿAmmār ⚜ and the water in the form of a black slave and God gave victory to ʿAmmār ⚜ over him." ʿAli ⚜ said, "We met ʿAmmār ⚜ and informed him of what the Messenger of God ﷺ mentioned." He then said, "By God, had I known that he was a devil, I would have killed him." (*Abū al-Shaykh ibn Hayyān-Kitab al-ʿAzam, Abū Nuʿaym – Dalāil and Mʿarūf as-Sahābah*)

The last four narrations (6, 7, 8 and 9) all inform us of Satan being wrestled in human form. In the Islamic tradition, Iblīs (Satan) is from the species of Jinn, "a species of the unseen real realm, concealed from humans, though humans are not concealed from them."[136]

The traditions highlight the wrestling and martial ability of the Companions ⚜ in such encounters.

---

136 Hamza Yusuf, *The Creed of Imam-al-Tahawi*, (Zaytuna Institute, 2007), p.113.

الحديث العاشر

قَالَ ابْنُ سَعْدٍ فِي «الطَّبَقَاتِ»: «لَـمَّا خَرَجَ رَسُوْلُ/النَّبِيُّ إِلَى أُحُدٍ وَعَرَضَ أَصْحَابَهُ فَرَدَّ مَنِ اسْتَصْغَرَ، رَدَّ سَمُرَةَ بْنَ جُنْدُبٍ، وَأَجَازَ رَافِعَ بْنَ خَدِيْجٍ. فَقَالَ سَمُرَةُ لِرَبِيْبِهِ مُرِيِّ بْنِ سِنَانَ: «يَا أَبَتِ، أَجَازَ رَسُوْلُ اللهِ صَلَّى اللهُ عَلَيْهِ وَسَلَّمَ رَافِعَ بْنَ خَدِيْجٍ وَرَدَّنِي، وَأَنَا أَصْرَعُ رَافِعَ بْنَ خَدِيْجٍ». فَقَالَ مُرِيُّ بْنُ سِنَانَ: «يَا رَسُوْلَ اللهِ! رَدَدْتَ ابْنِيْ وَأَجَزْتَ رَافِعَ بْنَ خَدِيْجٍ وَابْنِي يَصْرَعُهُ»، فَقَالَ النَّبِيُّ صَلَّى اللهُ عَلَيْهِ وَسَلَّمَ لِرَافِعٍ وَسَمُرَةَ: «تَصَارَعَا»، فَصَرَعَ سَمُرَةُ رَافِعًا، فَأَجَازَهُ رَسُوْلُ اللهِ صَلَّى اللهُ عَلَيْهِ وَسَلَّمَ فِي أُحُدٍ، فَشَهِدَهَا مَعَ الْمُسْلِمِيْنَ.

(أخرجه ابن سعد في «الطبقات»)

Ibn Saʿd 🙵 mentioned in his al-Ṭabaqāt: When the Prophet 🙵 set off for (the Battle of) Uḥud and inspected his companions, returning those whom he deemed too young, he 🙵 returned Samurah ibn Jundub 🙵 and permitted Rāfiʿ ibn Khadīj 🙵. So Samurah said to his foster father Muriyy ibn Sinān, "O father! the Messenger of God 🙵 gave permission to Rāfiʿ ibn Khadīj and returned me, whereas I can defeat Rāfiʿ ibn Khadīj." So Muriyy ibn Sinān said, "O Messenger of God 🙵, you returned my son and permitted Rāfiʿ ibn Khadīj whereas my son can take him down." So the Prophet 🙵 said to Rāfiʿ and Samurah, "Wrestle each other." And so

Samurah took Rāfi‘ down. The Messenger of God ﷺ gave him permission for Uḥud, and thus he participated with the Muslims. (*Ibn Sa‘d – Tabaqāt*)

In the lead up to the Battle of Uḥud, on 5 Shawwal 3AH, the Messenger of God ﷺ requested his Companions to track the movement of the Quraysh as they approached the city of Medīnah. It was reported that the army of the Quraysh had moved close to Medīnah and that the illuminated city was in danger of being attacked. So, sentinel guards were designated and posted along the frontiers; most notably Sa‘d ibn ‘Ubāda ﷺ and Sa‘d ibn Mu‘ādh ﷺ stood guard by the door of the *Masjid an-Nabawī* (the Prophet's Mosque), armed with their weaponry for the entire night. The following morning the Messenger of God ﷺ consulted his Companions ﷺ on their opinion about advancing for battle, to which two proposals were suggested:

i. Many of the senior Migrants and Helpers suggested that the womenfolk be sent to forts outside the city and that they should defend the city from within, a view endorsed by one ‘Abd Allāh ibn Ubayy, who, whilst being a chieftain of the Banū Khazraj, had never before been a party to consultation.

ii. The younger Companions ﷺ, who had not participated in the Battle of Badr, insisted on advancing outside of the city and attacking the Quraysh.

Upon hearing this the Prophet ﷺ walked swiftly to his home and returned donning his full armour; the Companions at that moment apologised for compelling the Prophet ﷺ to adopt their suggestion and attempted to retract their opinion, to which the Prophet ﷺ said, "It is not fitting that a Prophet who has put on his armour should lay it aside until he has fought."[137]

---

137 A. Guillaume, *The Life of Muhammad – A translation of Ishaq's Sirat Rasul God* (Oxford University Press, 1955), p.372.

The Quraysh reached the outskirts of the city of Medīnah and set up camp on Wednesday, with the Prophet ﷺ marching out, having offered the Friday prayer with a thousand Companions. This was reduced to seven hundred as ʿAbd Allāh ibn Ubayy retracted three hundred of his men out of spite, due to his suggestion not being adopted. Of the remaining Companions prepped for battle, only a hundred wore armour due to lack of resources.

A final review of the battalion was undertaken by the Messenger of God ﷺ, with a number of Companions being sent back due to their young age. These included the likes of Zayd ibn Thābit, Abū Saʿīd al-Khudrī, ʿAbd Allāh ibn ʿUmar, Barāʾ ibn ʿĀzib and ʿAraba ibn Aws, who was only fourteen years old at the time.

It was here that Rāfiʿ ibn Khadīj, selected primarily for masterful archery skills, was asked to grapple with Samurah ibn Jundub, with the latter subsequently threw him down.

الحديث الحادي عشر

عَنْ سَمُرَةَ بْنِ جُنْدُبٍ، قَالَ: «كَانَ النَّبِيُّ صَلَّى اللهُ عَلَيْهِ وَسَلَّمَ
يَعْرِضُ غِلْمَانَ الأَنْصَارِ فِي كُلِّ عَامٍ، فَمَنْ بَلَغَ مِنْهُمْ بَعَثَهُ،
فَعَرَضَهُمْ ذَاتَ عَامٍ، فَمَرَّ بِهِ غُلَامٌ فَبَعَثَهُ فِي الْبَعْثِ، وَعَرَضَ
عَلَيْهِ سَمُرَةُ مِنْ بَعْدِهِ فَرَدَّهُ. فَقَالَ سَمُرَةُ: «يَا رَسُولَ اللهِ، أَجَزْتَ
غُلَامًا وَرَدَدْتَنِي، وَلَوْ صَارَعَنِي لَصَرَعْتُهُ». فَقَالَ: «فَدُونَكَ
فَصَارِعْهُ». قَالَ: «فَصَرَعْتُهُ»، فَأَجَازَنِي فِي الْبَعْثِ.

(أخرجه الطبراني في «المعجم الكبير» والحاكم في
«المستدرك»، كذا في المسارعة)

The Prophet ﷺ would inspect the young men of the
Anṣār every year. Whoever amongst them attained
maturity, he ﷺ would accept for military service.
During an inspection one year, a young man passed
by him ﷺ and he ﷺ sent him to join the army. Then
Samurah was assessed by him ﷺ thereafter but was
rejected. Samurah thus said, "O Messenger of God ﷺ,
you permitted a young man but rejected me, whereas
if he was to wrestle me I would defeat him." He ﷺ said,
"Go and wrestle him." He said, "So I took him down. He
ﷺ thus permitted me to join the army." (al-Tabarāni –
Mu'jam al Kabīr, al-Hākim – Mustadrak)

الحديث الثاني عشر

عَنْ عَبْدِ الرَّحْمَنِ بْنِ أَبِيْ نُعْمٍ أَنَّ أَبَا سَعِيْدٍ سُئِلَ عَنِ الصَّلَاةِ فِي الثَّوْبِ. فَقَالَ: «تَتَّزِرُ بِهِ كَمَا تَتَّزِرُ لِلصِّرَاعِ».

(رواه ابن أبي شيبة في «المصنف»، كذا في المسارعة)

On the authority of ʿAbd ar-Raḥmān ibn Abī Nuʿmin relates that, Abū Saʿīd (al-Khudri) ﷺ was asked about performing prayer in one cloth. So, he said, "Wrap it just as you wrap it for wrestling." (*Ibn Abī Shaybah – Muṣannaf*)

ʿAbd al-Raḥmān ibn Abī Nuʿmin was of the followers (*Tābiʿ*), an ascetic from Kufa, Iraq. He was locked in a house by Hajjāj ibn Yusuf for fifteen days, after which Hajjāj returned to open thinking he had died but found him in prayer.

Abū Saʿid, Saʿd ibn Mālik ibn Sinān ibnʿUbayd ibn Thaʿlabah ibn al-Abjar, Khudrah ibnʿAwf ibn aḷ-Hārith ibn al-Khazraj al-Ansāri, known as Abū Saʿīd al-Khudri is the famous companion who offered himself to fight in the Battle of Uḥud at age 13. Although was deemed too young to fight, he witnessed his father, Mālik ibn Sinān, martyred in the same battle. A renowned warrior, he fought in all the wars of prophethood thereafter, starting with the Battle of Khandaq, when he was just 15 years of age. A prolific narrator of prophetic traditions, narrating 1,170 traditions of the Messenger of God ﷺ, he died on Jumuʿah and is buried in al-Baqīʿ.[138]

---

138 Adapted from Ibn Sayyid'n Nās, *Light of the Eyes – An Abridgement of the Biography of the Trusted, The Trustworthy* – translated by Ibrahim Osi-Efa, (Furthest Boundary Press, 2020).

This narration provides a degree of clarity as to the attire of the grapplers at the time of the Messenger of God ﷺ. It was known for men amongst the Companions ﷺ who through poverty did not possess sufficient clothing to adequately dress themselves, to barely have enough cloth to cover their *'awra* (nakedness).[139] As this narration indicates, grapplers would use a single cloth (*izār*) to wrap their lower body and remain bare-chested, sufficiently covering their nakedness and meeting the minimum requirement for prayer. The narration also indicates a familiarity and regular practice of wrestling amongst the Companions.

Salama ibn al-Akwaʿ ﷺ[140] said: "'Uthmān ibn 'Affān's wrap-around would reach to the midway of his shins. He would say: 'This was the wrapround of my companion'. Meaning the Prophet ﷺ."[141]

In a well-known tradition, a companion called upon the Messenger of God ﷺ whilst he was at his aunt's residence. He answered the door bare-chested, with only a lower body wrapper.

In a related tradition we find another narration of the Prophet ﷺ wrestling Rukānah ﷺ, who then further clarifies a matter of Muslim attire:

عَنْ أَبِي جَعْفَرِ بْنِ مُحَمَّدِ بْنِ عَلِيِّ بْنِ رُكَانَةَ، عَنْ أَبِيهِ، أَنَّ رُكَانَةَ،

صَارَعَ النَّبِيَّ صلى الله عليه وسلم فَصَرَعَهُ النَّبِيُّ صلى الله عليه

وسلم قَالَ رُكَانَةُ وَسَمِعْتُ النَّبِيَّ صلى الله عليه وسلم يَقُولُ

---

139 The minimum of one's body to be covered in order to fulfil a condition of the prayer. Whilst there are slight differences between the four canonical schools of jurisprudence in Islam as to what this constitutes, the general consensus for men is to cover at minimum from their navel to their knees.

140 Salama ibn al-Akwaʿ, a tremendous soldier from amongst the Companions, participating in seven military campaigns with the Messenger of God ﷺ, nine with Abū Bakr ﷺ and once with Usāma ibn Zayd ﷺ. Known as a master archer and possessing incredible sprinting abilities. In a narration found in Sahih Muslim, during the battle of Hawazin, a camel stolen by a spy bolted from the encampment, Salama ibn al-Akwaʿ gave chase outrunning the camel and finally grabbing the nose ring of the beast and bringing it back. God be pleased with him.

141 Thaqib Mahmood, *The Perfect Paragon Muhammad – A Summation of Imam Al-Tirmidhi's Al-Shama'il al-Muhammadiyyah* (CEI, 2011) p.18.

« فَرْقُ مَا بَيْنَنَا وَبَيْنَ الْمُشْرِكِينَ الْعَمَائِمُ عَلَى الْقَلَانِسِ » .

On the authority of Abī Jaʿfar ibn Muḥammad ibn ʿAli
ibn Rukānah quoting his father said: Rukānah wrestled
with the Prophet ﷺ and the Prophet ﷺ took him
down. Rukānah said: I heard the Prophet ﷺ say: "The
difference between us and the polytheists is that we wear
turbans over our caps."[142]

Later scholars would also adopt similar attire when engaging in the Prophetic arts, attempting to draw close to God, as
is related by Abū Bakr Zāhid as-Samarqandī[143] who mentions,

I spent a night with Imam al-Lāmishī[144] in some of his
gardens; he left from one of the gates of the garden
midway through the night and he went along his way.
So I stood up and followed him from where he couldn't
see me. He reached a large, deep river. Removing his
clothes, he put on a sarong waist wrap (izār) and then
dived into the water. He remained under water for
a while. As his head did not come up for some time I
felt he had drowned and immediately began shouting,
"O Muslims, the Shaykh has drowned!". After a short
amount of time, indeed he reappeared from beneath the
water. He said, "O my son, don't worry." I said, "O my
master, I thought you had drowned!" He said, "I did not
drown, however I intended to prostate to God on a piece
of earth within this river because I indeed believe that
no one has prostrated on this (part of earth) for God."[145]

142 Abū Dawūd – Sunan 4078, al-Tirmidhī – Jāmiʿ 1784.
143 Abu Bakr Zāhid as-Samarqandī "was a Ḥanafī theologian and jurist in the tradition of
Abū Manṣūr al-Māturīdī (d. c. 333/944). Despite his apparent renown in later centuries and the
authority accorded to him to this day as an interpreter of Islamic law, very little concrete information
about his life and work is preserved." (taken from https://referenceworks.brillonline.com/entries/
encyclopaedia-of-islam-3/*-COM_26318)
144 Abū al-Thanā Maḥmūd ibn Zayd al-Lāmishī was a Hanafī-Maturidi scholar from Transoxiana
(from Lamish in Fergana in modern Uzbekistan) of the late 5th and 6th Islamic centuries. He penned
the work Kitāb Fī Uṣūl al Fiqh, which apparently "is unique amongst works of the usul al-fiqh genre
of literature. Unlike other texts, it is arranged more like a glossary and less in accordance with the
classic scheme of subject-division in usul books. The definitions and explanations offered by the
author are surprisingly simple, easy to understand, and void of the complex linguistic constructions
that would be become characteristic of later works." (taken from https://attahawi.com/)
145 al-Jawāhir al-Muḍiyya fī al-Tabaqāt-al Hanafiyya – A Biography of the Hanafi Scholars.

الحديث الثالث عشر

عَنِ ابْنِ عَبَّاسٍ قَالَ: «كَانَ أَهْلُ مَكَّةَ لَا يُسَابِقُهُمْ أَحَدٌ إِلَّا
سَبَقُوْهُ وَلَا يُصَارِعُهُمْ أَحَدٌ إِلَّا صَرَعُوْهُ حَتَّى رَغِبُوْا عَنْ مَاءِ
زَمْزَمَ».

(أخرجه أبو ذر الهروي في «المنسك»)

On the authority of Ibn ʿAbbās ﷺ said that, No one
used to race the people of Mecca except they used to
beat them, and no one used to wrestle them except
they would defeat them. (This was the case) until they
turned away from the water of Zam Zam. (*Abū Dharr
al-Harawī*)

Scholars indicate that the Meccans "turning away from the
water of Zam Zam" relates to a state of arrogance that developed
on account of their strength, to the point they stopped using Zam
Zam water to fulfil their needs.

عَنِ ابْنِ عَبَّاسٍ رَضِيَ اللهُ تَعَالَى عَنْهُمَا، قَالَ: «كَانَ أَهْلُ مَكَّةَ
لَا يَشْتَكُوْنَ رُكَبَهُمْ، وَلا يُسَابِقُوْنَ أَحَدًا إِلَّا سَبَقُوْهُ.
وَلَا يُصَارِعُوْنَ أَحَدًا إِلَّا صَرَعُوْهُ، حَتَّى رَغِبُوْا عَنْ مَاءِ زَمْزَمَ،
فَـبَدَّلَ بِهِمْ.

Al-Fākihī[146] quotes the same narration (above) with the addition in the beginning that *"they did not have any complaints about their riding animals."* Murtada Zabīdī[147] in his commentary on Imam al-Ghazali's *Ihya Ulūm ad-Dīn* quotes the same narration from Abū Dharr al-Harawi with the addition *"because of this, they were afflicted with an illness in their feet."*

This hadith is narrated by none other than the great scholar of the Companions, 'Abd Allāh ibn 'Abbās, cousin of the Messenger of God ﷺ. Meccans were known for their athletic abilities, particularly their accuracy in archery, ability to sprint and their wrestling prowess.

God mentions with regards to the brothers of Prophet Yusuf ﷺ, who mentioned to their father Prophet Ya'qūb ﷺ that

$$ \text{قَالُواْ يَٰٓأَبَانَآ إِنَّا ذَهَبْنَا نَسْتَبِقُ ۝ ١٢:١٧} $$

They say "O our father, indeed we went racing each other..."
(Quran, 12:17)

The great 7th century Quran commentator, Fakhr al-Dīn al-Rāzī ﷺ, explains that this verse was the claim the brothers made to adequately train for combatting enemies and wolves.[148]

As previously mentioned, several of the Companions ﷺ were renowned for their sprinting abilities; perhaps the most well-known race was the beautiful, playful one between the Messenger of God ﷺ and his beloved wife 'Ā'isha ﷺ:

$$ \text{عَنْ عَائِشَةَ رَضِيَ اللهُ تَعَالَى عَنْهَا، أَنَّهَا كَانَتْ مَعَ النَّبِيِّ صَلَّى} $$

---

146 Abu 'Abd Allah Muhammad ibn Ishaq ibn al-'Abbas al-Fākihi - born 215–220 AH; died 272-279 AH, was an eminent historian and hadith scholar of Mecca. He narrated ahadith from preeminent hadith scholars such as Muhammad Ibn Ismail al-Bukhari, Muslim ibn al-Hajjaj, Abu Hatim al-Razi and Abu Zur'ah Jurjani.

147 Muḥammad ibn Muḥammad Murtaḍá al-Zabīdī was an Islamic scholar 1732–1790 (1145–1205AH), renowned author of the dictionary Taj al-Arus Min Jawahir al-Qamus and wrote a commentary on Imam Abu Hamid al-Ghazali's *Ihya Ulūm ad-Din*. Born in Bilgram Hardoi district, Uttar Pradesh, India, his family originated from Wasit in Iraq, from where his parents had emigrated to the Hadramawt region in the east of Yemen. Murtada earned his *Nisba 'al-Zabīdī'* from Zabīd in the south western coastal plains of Yemen, which was a centre of academic learning where he had spent time studying. He died in Egypt during a plague in 1790 (1205AH).

148 Seyyed Hossein Nasr, *The Study Quran*, (Harper Collins, 2015), p.596.

اللهُ عَلَيْهِ وَسَلَّمَ فِي سَفَرٍ، قَالَتْ: فَسَابَقْتُهُ، فَسَبَقْتُهُ عَلَى رِجْلَيَّ. فَلَمَّا حَمَلْتُ اللَّحْمَ سَابَقْتُهُ فَسَبَقَنِي، فَقَالَ: «هَذِهِ بِتِلْكَ السَّبْقَةِ.

I had a race with him and I outstripped him on my feet. When I became fleshy, (again) I had a race with him ﷺ and he outstripped me." He ﷺ said: "This is for that outstripping."[149]

---

149   Sunan Abi Dawud 2578.

الحديث الرابع عشر

عَنْ أَبِيْ جَعْفَرٍ قَالَ: «اصْطَرَعَ الْحَسَنُ وَالْحُسَيْنُ»، فَقَالَ رَسُوْلُ
اللهِ صَلَّى اللهُ عَلَيْهِ وَسَلَّمَ: «هِيَ حَسَنٌ»، فَقَالَتْ فَاطِمَةُ: «كَأَنَّهُ
أَحَبَّ إِلَيْكَ»، قَالَ: «لَا، وَلَكِنَّ جِبْرِيْلَ يَقُوْلُ: «هِيَ حُسَيْنٌ».

(أخرجه ابن أبي شيبة في «المصنف»)

On the authority of Abū Ja'far (Muhammad ibn 'Ali ibn
Husayn ibn Ali ibn Abū Tālib) said that, Hasan ﷺ and
Husayn ﷺ wrestled each other. The Messenger of God
ﷺ said, "Come on Hasan!" Fatimah ﷺ said, "It seems
he is more beloved to you?" He ﷺ replied, "No, it is
because Gabriel is saying, 'Come on Husayn!'" (*Ibn Abī
Shaybah – Muṣannaf*)

This narration is on the authority of Muhammad ibn 'Ali
ibn Husayn ibn Ali ibn Abū Tālib, also known as Abū Ja'far or
al-Bāqir born in 57AH and died in 114AH.

This vivid scene shows the playful nature of the Best of
Creation ﷺ as he encourages his grandchildren in their grappling
bout, with their beloved mother Fatimah ﷺ looking on. This
deeply instructive narration encourages play with children and
proves grappling a worthwhile practice, particularly in relation to
children[150] and positive reinforcement. There is no indication of
the ages of Hasan ﷺ and Husayn ﷺ at the time of this narration;
it is safe to say they were both under eight years of age given that
they were eight and seven years old respectively upon the demise
of the Prophet ﷺ in 11AH.

150   Albeit the narration does not clarify the respective ages of al-Hasan and al-Husayn.

Today, parents (and by extension, grandparents) are increasingly absent from the activities and interests of their children, with an almost "hands-off" approach to extracurricular sports, not least due to the decreasing rate of health among most adults. The prevailing attitude amongst parents who do enrol their children in the martial arts is often one of "do as I say, not as I do", with many living vicariously through their children and pushing their own high aspirations and expectations onto them. This places undue stress and pressure upon young, impressionable minds and bodies. In some instances, there can be an overemphasis on participating in competitive team sports, of which the embedded culture and underlying objectives—to win at any cost—corrupts the innocent and fertile minds of the youth, leading to a type of hooliganism deprived of virtue. This appears contrary to the way of the Messenger of God ﷺ as this narration indicates.

Interesting studies also provide validity and demonstrate countless benefits to the time-old family tradition of "roughhousing" that the above narration alludes to,

> Roughhousing is play that flows with spontaneity, improvisation, and joy. It is free from worries about how we look… It is physical, and it promotes physical fitness, release of tension, and well-being. Roughhousing is interactive, so it builds close connections between children and parents, especially as we get down on the floor and join them in their world of exuberance and imagination. Most important, roughhousing is rowdy, but not dangerous. With safety in mind, roughhousing releases the creative life force within each person, pushing us out of our inhibitions and inflexibilities.[151]

---

151 Anthony Benedet & Lawrence Cohen, *The Art of Roughhousing: Good Old-Fashioned Horseplay and Why Every Kid Needs it*, (Quirk Books, 2011), p.11.

الحديث الخامس عشر

عَنْ أَبِي هُرَيْرَةَ قَالَ: «كَانَ الْحَسَنُ وَالْحُسَيْنُ يَصْطَرِعَانِ بَيْنَ
يَدَيْ رَسُولِ اللهِ صَلَّى اللهُ عَلَيْهِ وَسَلَّمَ»، فَكَانَ رَسُولُ اللهِ صَلَّى
اللهُ عَلَيْهِ وَسَلَّمَ يَقُولُ: «هِيَ حَسَنٌ»، فَقَالَتْ فَاطِمَةُ: «يَا رَسُولَ
اللهِ، لِمَ تَقُولُ: «هِيَ حَسَنٌ»؟ فَقَالَ: «إِنَّ جِبْرِيْلَ يَقُولُ: «هِيَ
حُسَيْنٌ».

(أخرجه الحسن بن سفيان في «المسند» وأبو نعيم في «فضائل
الصحابة» وابن عساكر، كذا في المسارعة)

On the authority of Abū Hurayrah ﷺ said that, Hasan
ﷺ and Husayn ﷺ were wrestling before the Messenger
of God ﷺ. The Messenger of God ﷺ was saying, "Come
on Hasan." Fatimah ﷺ asked, "O Messenger of God,
why do you say 'Come on Al-Hasan?'" He ﷺ replied,
"Gabriel is saying 'Come on Husayn.'" (al-Hasan ibn
Sufyan – Musnad Nasawi, Abū Nuʿaym – Fadail as
Sahābah, Ibn ʿAsākir)

NARRATION 16

الحديث السادس عشر

عَنْ عَلِيِّ بْنِ أَبِي طَالِبٍ قال: «تَعَدَّ رَسُولُ اللهِ صَلَّى اللهُ عَلَيْهِ
وَسَلَّمَ مَوْضِعَ الْـجَنَائِزِ وَأَنَا مَعَهُ، فَطَلَعَ الْـحَسَنُ والْـحُسَيْنُ،
فَاصْطَرَعَا، فَقَالَ النَّبِيُّ صَلَّى اللهُ عَلَيْهِ وَسَلَّمَ: «إِيْهًا حَسَنُ خُذْ
حُسَيْنًا»، فَقَالَ عَلِيٌّ: «يَا رَسُولَ اللهِ: أَعَلَى الْـحُسَيْنِ تُوَالِيْهِ؟»
فَقَالَ: «هَذَا جِبْرِيْلُ يَقُوْلُ: إِيْهًا حُسَيْنُ».

(أخرجه ابن عساكر في تاريخه، كذا في المسارعة)

On the authority of 'Alī ibn Abī Ṭālib ﷺ said that, The
Messenger of God ﷺ passed the area of funerals and I
was with him. Hasan ﷺ and Husayn ﷺ appeared and
began wrestling. The Prophet ﷺ said, "Go on Hasan,
take Husayn!" So 'Ali ﷺ said, "O Messenger of God, are
you supporting him over Husayn?" He ﷺ said, "Gabriel
over here is saying, 'Go on Husayn!'" (*Ibn 'Asākir –
Tārikh*)

الحديث السابع عشر

عَنْ عُرْوَةَ رُوَيْمٍ قَالَ: «جَاءَ أَعْرَابِيٌّ إِلَى النَّبِيِّ صَلَّى اللهُ عَلَيْهِ
وَسَلَّمَ فَقَالَ: «يَا رَسُولَ اللهِ، صَارِعْنِي؟» فَقَامَ إِلَيْهِ مُعَاوِيَةُ،
فَقَالَ: «يَا أَعْرَابِيُّ، أَنَا أُصَارِعُكَ»، فَقَالَ النَّبِيُّ صَلَّى اللهُ عَلَيْهِ
وَسَلَّمَ: «لَنْ يُغْلَبَ مُعَاوِيَةُ أَبَدًا، فَصُرِعَ الْأَعْرَابِيُّ، فَلَمَّا كَانَ
يَوْمُ صِفِّينٍ، قَالَ عَلِيٌّ: «لَوْ ذَكَرْتُ هَذَا الْحَدِيثَ مَا قَاتَلْتُ
مُعَاوِيَةَ».

(أخرجه ابن عساكر، كذا في المسارعة)

On the authority of 'Urwa (ibn) Ruwaym said that, A
bedouin came to the Prophet 鹵 and said, "O Messenger
of God, wrestle me." So Mu'āwiyah 鹵 came towards
him and said, "O Bedouin, I will wrestle you." So the
Prophet 鹵 said, "Mu'āwiyah will never be beaten." Then
the bedouin was taken down. When it was the day of
Siffīn, 'Alī 鹵 said, "If I had recalled this tradition, I
would not have fought Mu'āwiyah." (*Ibn 'Asākir*)

Through scholarly consultation, there does not appear to
be anyone known as "Urwa Ruwaym". However, Ibn Asākir in
Tarikh Dimishq mentions Urwa and Ruwaym as two separate
individuals. Additionally, the abridgement (*mukhtasar*) of the
same work identifies 'Urwa *ibn* Ruwaym—who we believe is
the one being referred to in this narration—as a follower (*Tābi'*)
who passed away in 140AH, suggesting a potential typographical
error in the Arabic edition used.

The Battle of Siffīn (Safar 37AH–May/July 657) occurred during the First *Fitna*, or first Muslim civil war. It was fought between 'Ali ibn Abī Tālib ﷺ who ruled as the Fourth Caliph and Mu'āwiyah I, over avenging the murder of the Third Caliph, Uthmān ibn Affān ﷺ. This took place on the banks of the Euphrates river, in modern-day Raqqa, Syria.

الحديث الثامن عشر

عَنِ ابْنِ عَبَّاسٍ، قَالَ: «جَاءَ أَعْرَابِيٌّ إِلَى النَّبِيِّ صَلَّى اللهُ عَلَيْهِ
وَسَلَّمَ فَقَالَ: «قُمْ يَا مُعَاوِيَةُ، فَصَارِعْهُ»، فَقَامَ فَصَارَعَهُ، فَصَرَعَهُ
مُعَاوِيَةُ، فَقَالَ النَّبِيُّ صَلَّى اللهُ عَلَيْهِ وَسَلَّمَ: «إِنَّ مُعَاوِيَةَ لَا
يُصَارِعُ أَحَدًا إِلَّا صَرَعَهُ مُعَاوِيَةُ».

(أخرجه الديلمي في «مسند الفردوس»)

On the authority of Ibn 'Abbās ﷺ said that, A bedouin
came to the Prophet ﷺ and he said, "Stand, O Mu'āwiyah
and wrestle him." So, he stood and wrestled him. Then
Mu'āwiyah ﷺ took him down and the Prophet ﷺ
said, "Mu'āwiyah does not wrestle anybody except that
Mu'āwiyah defeats them." (al-Daylami)

An endorsement beyond measure, the Messenger of God ﷺ
highlights the great grappling abilities of the noble Companion
Mu'āwiyah ibn Abī Sufyān ﷺ, who shares a lineage with the
Messenger of God ﷺ through having the same great-great
grandfather, Abd' Manāf ibn Qusay. He embraced Islam at the
Opening of Mecca alongside his parents and brother. He went
on to become governor of the Levant, thereafter becoming the
caliph whose reign lasted twenty years, which initiated the start
of the Umayyad dynasty until his death in Damascus in 60AH.

May God bless our master Muhammad ﷺ, his family and
his Companions and may He grant them always much peace
which is everlasting.

BIBLIOGRAPHY

A. Rahman Zaky – *A Preliminary Bibliography of Medieval Arabic Military Literature* (Consejo Superior de Investigaciones Científicas, 1965)

Ahmad Mubarak & Dawud Walid, *Centering Black Narrative – Black Muslim Nobles Among the Early Pious Muslims - vol.1 & Ahl al-Bayt, Blackness & Africa - vol.2* (Itrah Press 2016, 2018)

Akram, A.I, *Sword of God - Khalid bin al-Waleed* (Maktabah Publishers & Distributors, 2004)

Al-Jawziyya, Ibn al-Qayyim, *al-Dā' wa al-Dawā' – Spiritual Disease and Its Cure* (Al-Firdous Ltd, 2006)

Al-Ghazali, Abu Hamid, *Al-Ghazali on Disciplining the Soul & on Breaking the Two Desires: Books XXII and XXIII of the Revival of the Religious Sciences – translated by T.J. Winter* (Islamic Texts Society, 1995)

'Ali ibn Ahmad al Wahīdi, *Al-Wahidi's Asbab Al-nuzul: v. 3: The Great Commentaries of the Holy Qur'an* (Fons Vitae, 2009)

Al-Kadi, Abdullah H., *Mecca To Madinah – A Photographic Journey of the Hijrah Route* (Orient East, 2013)

Al-Qaradawi, Yusuf, *The Lawful and the Prohibited in Islam.* (Al-Birr Foundation, 2003)

al-Sarraf, Shihab. "Mamluk Furusiyah Literature and Its Antecedents." *The Middle East Documentation Center (MEDOC)*, University of Chicago (2004): 200.

Alter, Adam, *Irresistible* (Bodley Head, 2017)

Alter, Joseph S, *The Wrestler's Body* (University of California Press, 1992)

Anthony Benedet & Lawrence Cohen, *The Art of Roughhousing: Good Old-Fashioned Horseplay and Why Every Kid Needs it* (Quirk Books, 2011)

Bemath, Yusuf, *Al-Asl – The Pure-bred Arabian* (Impress Investments Ltd, 2012)

Bodycomb, Reilly Asher, *Sambo Wrestling* (CreateSpace Independent Publishing Platform, 2012)

Bouhdiba, Abdelwahab/ M. Maruf Al-Dawalibi, *The Individual and Society in Islam* (Unesco Publication. 1998)

Butt, Abdullah, *Aspects of Shah Ismail Shaheed – Essays on his literary political and religious activities* (Qaum Kutub Khana, Lahore 1943)

Carroll, Scott T. "Wrestling in Ancient Nubia." *Journal of Sport History*, 15, no. 2 (1988): 121–37

Cornell, Svante, *Small Nations and Great Powers – A study of the ethnopolitical conflict in the Caucasus* (Curzon Press, 2001)

Danaher, John/ Gracie, Renzo, *Mastering Jujitsu*. Human Kinetics. 2003

David Nicolle, Christa Hook, *Saracen Faris* (Reed International Books, 1994)

Dever, Ayhan "Sports Lodges in the Ottoman Empire Depicted in the Travel Book (Seyahat-Name) of Evliya Çelebi." *Annals of Applied Sport Science*, 7 (2019): 49

Donner, Fred, *The Early Islamic Conquests*, (Princeton University Press, 1981)

Faizer, Rizwi, *The Life of Muhammad – Al-Waqidi's Kitab al-Maghazi*, (Routledge, 2011)

Guillaume, A, *The Life of Muhammad – A translation of Ishaq's Sirat Rasul God* (Oxford University Press, 1955)

Haddad, Gibril Fouad, *Sports in Islam* - http://steppenreiter.de/sports_in_islam.htm

Haddad, Gibril Fouad, *The Four Imams and their Schools* (Muslim Academic Trust, 2007)

Hall, Mark, *The Pyjama Game* (Aurum Press Ltd, 2008)

Hedges, Chris, *Empire of Illusion – The End of Literacy and the Triumph of Spectacle* (Nation Books, 2009)

Holiday, Ryan, *Ego is the Enemy* (Profile Books Ltd, 2016)

Hourani, Albert, *A History of the Arab Peoples* (Faber & Faber Ltd, 1991)

Hugh Kennedy, *The Armies of the Caliphs* (Routledge, 2001)

Hugh Kennedy, *The Great Arab Conquests: How Islam Changed the World We Live In* (Da Capo Press, 2008)

Ibn Kathir, *The Life of Prophet Muhammad - Al-Sira al Nabawiyya - Volume 1 – translated by Professor Trevor Le Gassick* (Garnet Publishing, 1998)

Ibn Sayyid an Nās, *Light of the Eyes – An Abridgement of the Biography of the Trusted, The Trustworthy – translated by Ibrahim Osi-Efa* (Furthest Boundary Press, 2020)

Imam Abdul Wahhab Ash-Sha'rani – *The Muhammadan Covenants* (get reference)

Imam al-Waqidi, *The Islamic Conquest of Syria.* (Ta-Ha Publishers Ltd. 2009)

J.M.Cowan, *The Hans Wehr Dictionary of Modern Written Arabic* (Spoken Language Services, 1976)

Jabali, Fuad, *The Companions of the Prophet – A Study of Geographical Distribution and Political Arguments* (Brill, 2003)

Jalal Ad-Din as-Suyūṭī, *Al-Arbaʿīn – On the Principles of Legal Judgements, Virtuous Actions, and Asceticism* (Turath Publishing, 2009)

Jarir al-Tabari, *History of al-Tabari vol.8 – Translated by Michael Fishbein* (State University of New York Press, 1997)

Jason Goodwin, *Lords of the Horizons – A History of the Ottoman Empire* (Vintage Books London, 2010)

Kameas, Nikolaos, Albanidis Evangelos & Barbas Ioannis "The Decency of Strength and the Strength of Decency: A Philosophical Approach to the Sport of Wrestling." International Journal of Wrestling Science , 6 (2016): 11–15.

Kano, Jigoro, *Mind Over Muscle – Writings from The Founder of Judo*. (Kodanshausa USA Inc 2013)

Keller, Dr Christia, *Intentional Ignorance? - USAWC, PME, and Middle Eastern Theory and History*. Strategy research paper. (USAWC. 2016)

Kennedy, Hugh, *The Armies of the Caliphs*. (Routledge. 2001)

Kennell, Nigel, *Gymnasium of Virtue: Education and Culture in Ancient Sparta*. (The University of North Carolina Press, 2007).

Khorasani, M. M, *Persian Archery and Swordsmanship: Historical Martial Arts of Iran* (Niloufer Books, 2013

Leonard, George, Mastery, *The Keys to Success and Long-term Fulfilment* (Penguin Group. 1992)

Levinson, David/ Christensen, Karen, *Encyclopedia of World Sport* (Oxford University Press. 1999)

Lings, Martin, *Muhammad, his life based on the earliest sources* (Islamic Texts Society, 1991)

Mahmood, Thaqib, *The Perfect Paragon Muhammad – A Summation of Imam Al-Tirmidhi's Al-Shama'il al-Muhammadiyyah* (CEI, 2011)

Matakas, Chris, *On Jiu-jitsu* (Build The Fire Publishing, 2017)

Mehmet Gul, Mehmet Turkmen, Abdullah Dogan & Aydogan Soyguden "Lost Tradition in Kirkpinar Oil Wrestling: Importance of Kispet and Ceremony of Kispet Wearing".

International Journal of Wrestling Science, 5 (2015): 1, 52–55.

Mohammad Hashim Kamali, *Principles of Islamic Jurisprudence* (The Islamic Texts Society, 2003)

Mohammed, Ghazi bin, *The Sacred Origin of Sports and Culture* (Fons Vitae, 1998)

Muhammad Hamidullah, *The Battlefields of the Prophet Muhammad - 4th Edition* (Kitab Bhavan, 1992)

Muhammad Ibn Saad. *Kitab at-Tabaqat al-Kabir – vol.8 – The Women of Madina* (Ta-Ha Publishers Ltd, 1995)

Muhammad ibn Saad. *Kitab al-Tabaqat al-Kabair-vol. 3. - The Companions of Badr* (Ta-Ha Publishers Ltd, 2018)

Muhammad Ilyas Abdul Ghani, *Pictorial History of Madinah Munawwarah* (Al Rasheed Printers, 2004)

Muhammad Manazir Ahsan, *Social Life under The Abbasids* (SOAS, University of London, 1973)

Muhammad Yusuf Kandhlawi, *Hayatus Sahabah – The Lives of the Sahabah – Vol1* (Islamic Book Service, 2010),

Mustafa Kani, Sacred Archery -translation of Telhis-i-resailat-i-rumat (Himma Press 2017)

Nabahani, Yusuf, *Wasa'il al-Wusul ila Shama'il al-Rasul – Muhammad His Character and Beauty* translated by Abdul Aziz Suraqah (Al-Madina Institute, 2015)

Nabhani, Yusuf, *Endless Nobility of the Ahl al Bayt* - translated by Arfan Shah. (Islamic Information Society, 2013)

Nadwi, Abu'l Hasan Ali, *Saviours of Islamic Spirit.* (White Thread Press, 2015)

Nadwi, Mohammad Akram, *al-Muhaddithat: The Women Scholars of Islam* (Interface Publications Ltd, 2013)

Nicolle, David, *The Armies of Islam – 7th – 11th Centuries* (Osprey, 1982)

Nicolle, David/ Hook, Christa, *Saracen Faris* (Reed International Books, 1994)

Nikolaos Kameas, Evangelos Albanidis & Ioannis Barbas, *The Decency of Strength and the Strength of Decency: A Philosophical Approach to the Sport of Wrestling* (International Journal of Wrestling Science, Aug 2016)

Nitobe, Inazo, *Bushido - The Soul of Japan 13th Edition 1908.* (Project Gutenburg, 2004)

Poliakoff, Michael B, *Combat Sports in the Ancient World: Competition, Violence, and Culture.* (Yale University Press, 1995)

Potts, Daniel T, *The Arabian Gulf in Antiquity: Volume II: From Alexander the Great to the Coming of Islam.* (Oxford University Press, 1990)

Reusing, Holly McClung, *The Language of Martial Arts: The Transformative Potential of Brazilian Jiu-jitsu through the Lens of Depth Psychology.* (ProQuest LLC, 2015)

Rippetoe, Mark, *Starting Strength* (The Aasgaard Company, 2011)

Ryan Holiday, *Ego is the Enemy* (Profile Books Ltd, 2016)

Salim T.S. Al-Hassani, *1001 Inventions – The Enduring Legacy of Muslim Civilisation* (National Geographic Society, 2012)

Sallabi, Dr. Ali. M, *'Ali ibn Abi Talib – Volume One & Two*, (International Islamic Publishing House, 2011)

Sarrafi, Khashayar "The Way of Traditional Persian Wrestling Styles." Pahlevani Research Institute (2019): 11.

Sax, Leonard, *Boys Adrift* (Basic Books, 2007)

Seyyed Hossein Nasr, *The Study Quran* (Harper Collins, 2015)

Shannon, Jake/ Robinson, Billy, *Physical Chess: My Life in Catch-as-Catch-Can Wrestling* (ECW Press, 2012)

Shaykh Seraj Hendricks, *Sport and Islam* - http://mysite.mweb.co.za/residents/mfj1/sport.htm

Shibli Nomani & Syed Suleman Nadwi, *Sirat-un-Nabi, Life of the Prophet* (Darul Ishaat, 2003)

Shibli Numani, *Al-Farooq - The life of Omar the Great - translated by Maulana Zafar Ali Khan* (Adam Publishers & Distributors, 2003)

Shihab al Sarraf, *Mamluk Furusiyah Literature and Its Antecedents* (Mamluk Studies Review, 2004)

Shihab al-Sarraf, *A Companion to Medieval Arms and Armour* (Boydell Press, 2008)

Stevens, John, *The Way of Judo* (Shambhala Publications Inc. 2013)

The Biography of the Prophet Muhammad - Abridged (Deen Intensive, 2012)

Thomas A. Green, *Martial Arts of the World: An Encyclopaedia of History and Innovation, Volume 2* (ABC-CLIO, 2010)

Thomson, Geoff, *The Art of Fighting without Fighting* (Summerdale Publishers Ltd, 1998)

Topkapi Palace Museum. *Pavilion of the Scared Relics – The Sacred Trusts* (Tughra Books, 2009)

Townshend, Charles, *The Oxford History of Modern War* (Oxford University Press, 2005)

Trower, Marcus, *The Last Wrestlers* (EBury Press, 2007)

Tzu, Sun, *Sun Tzu on the Art of War - translated by Lionel Giles* (Allandale Online Publishing, 2000)

Yusuf, Hamza, *Purification of the Heart* (Starlatch Press, 2004)

Yusuf, Hamza, *The Content of Character* (Sandala LLC, 2005)

Yusuf, Hamza, *The Creed of Imam-al-Tahawi* (Zaytuna Institute, 2007)

Milton Keynes UK
Ingram Content Group UK Ltd.
UKHW040655160324
439418UK00015B/139/J